I0171934

Book Two:

Maximum Saints
Make No Little Plans

Inspirational stories and drawings by incarcerated "Maximum Saints" and volunteers at Adams County Detention Facility, Brighton, Colorado.

Yong Hui V. McDonald

"I have been typing many of the testimonials for Chaplain McDonald for her latest *MAXIMUM SAINTS* book. I was so moved by the stories; some actually brought me to tears. But it's the passion that these inmates have for the love of their Savior that is absolutely remarkable."
— Lorri Huff, Program Department Library Assistant, Adams County Detention Facility

"*MAXIMUM SAINTS* stories show that God is working in His own way to bring the wounded and the lost into His loving care, and He is using these writers to make all of the world know of His grace. I have been honored to be one of the tools He has used to help convey the message."
— Laura Nokes Lang, Editor

"I was inspired by the stories of the *MAXIMUM SAINTS*. Seeing how God has worked in the lives of those saints brought a deep desire to stand in the light of Jesus, so He can set me free from the shackles of my sins."
— Steven Rodriguez, an inmate at Adams County Detention Facility

"*MAXIMUM SAINTS* stories provide a powerful witness to our loving God who brings light into darkness, forgiveness and healing to the hurting, hope where there is none, and new life to those who are ready to 'turn around'-indeed, to all of us."
— Rev. Linda Gertenbach, Peace with Justice Facilitator, Rocky Mountain Conference of The United Methodist Church

"MAXIMUM SAINTS stories are witnessing power of the Holy Spirit in the lives of those Jesus came to free. This book is a blessing to each one who has written it, and to each one who has read it. We can only guess the ways in which each of us who read these pages will be inspired to reach out with a new sense of community."
— Rev. Miriam Siejko, Trinity United Methodist Church, Denver, Colorado

MAXIMUM SAINTS MAKE NO LITTLE PLANS

Copyright © Yong Hui V. McDonald also known as Vescinda McDonald. All Rights Reserved.
Produced by Transformation Project Prison Ministry (TPPM)
All rights reserved. No part of this publication may be reproduced, stored in a retrieval system, or transmitted in any form or by any means – electronic, mechanical, photocopying, recording, or otherwise – without the prior written permission from the copyright owners.

All Scripture quotations are taken from The Holy Bible, New International Version. Copyright © 1973, 1978, 1984 By International Bible Society. All Rights Reserved.

Printed in the United States of America
ISBN: 978-0-9825551-4-9
Cover drawing: Charles Polk, an inmate at ACDF
Cover Design: Lynette McClain
McClain Productions, www.mcclainproductions.com
First Printing: April 2007
Second Printing: November 2011
TPPM is a 501(c)(3) nonprofit corporation.
Transformation Project Prison Ministry
5209 Montview Boulevard, Denver, CO 80207
Website: www.maximumsaints.org
Facebook: http://tinyurl.com/yhhcp5g

Adams County Detention Facility inmates have given their consent to use their stories and illustrations in Maximum Saints books. Some authors and artists names have been changed by their request.

All the proceeds from *Maximum Saints* will go to TPPM to distribute more free books and DVDs to prisons and homeless shelters.

CONTENTS

DEDICATION
ACKNOWLEDGMENTS
INTRODUCTION

PART ONE: TESTIMONIALS

PART TWO: SERMONS AND MEDITATIONS

I dedicate this book to our Heavenly Father, our Lord Jesus, the Holy Spirit, and to all the incarcerated "Maximum Saints" all over the world whose hearts are serving Christ, saving souls and helping others.

Drawing "Dedication" by Burnie

Maximum saints are not necessarily classified as maximum inmates. I call them maximum saints because they use their gifts to the maximum to help others.

ACKNOWLEDGMENTS

My mother prays for me day and night. I thank God for my wonderful mother and her prayers. Because of her prayers, God granted me to see many miracles in my ministry!

My gratitude to all the following generous people who donated their time and gifts to make this book possible:

(1) All the ACDF inmates who contributed their stories.

(2) Drawings: Mr. Charles Polk and Burnie.

(3) Typing stories: Lori Huff, Maxine Maurie and Laura Lukes Lang.

(4) ACDF editors: Juanita Adams, Delores Bledsoe, Shawn Brady, Francesca Cayou, James Escalante, Stephanie Fuglestad, Felonis Hernandez, Amanda Powers, Perry Raymond, Julia Roberts, Lupe Rubio, Raelyn Santoya, Juanita Tamayo and Bernadette Warling.

(5) Art scans: Deputy Sheri Duran, Alvaro Duran and Jim Wickland.

(6) ACDF staff: Sheriff Douglas N. Darr, Captain James Wilbourn, Lieutenant David Shipley, Melanie Gregory, Technical Services Manager, Mr. Sterritt Fuller, Program Coordinator and all of the Program Department staff.

(7) Donors: The following churches and individuals graciously supported the Transformation Project Prison Ministry through funding: (1) Park Hill UMC 2) Broomfield UMC 3) Frontier UMC of Cheyenne Wyoming (4) Trinity UMC (5) Fort Lupton UMC (6) Brighton UMC (7) First Community UMC in Keenesburg (8) Westminster UMC (9) Northglenn UMC (10) Thornton UMC (11) Smoky Hill UMC (12) Jefferson Ave UMC (13) Grace UMC (14) Niwot UMC (15) First UMC, Fort Collins (16) Rocky Mountain Conference of UMC Peace With Justice (17) Foothills Christian Church (18) Northern Hills Christian Church (19) St. Stephens Lutheran Church in Northglenn (20) Resurrection Fellowship (21) All Nations Fellowship from Trinidad (22) First Love Christian Church (23) Love Outreach Pentecostal Church (24) Chaplain Sharon French from Larimer County Detention

Facility (25) Sara Choi (26) Hyon and David Bohnenkamp (27) Desmond McDonald (28) Hui Chae Lee (29) Sooja Oh (30) Son Hui Lee (31) Sandy Pietras (32) Rev. Sandy Blake (33) Rev. Don Marxhausen (34) House of Faith (35) Good Shepherd Community Church in Pueblo (35) Rev. Rebekah Simon-Peter (36) First United Methodist Church in Gillette, Wyoming. Some people donated anonymously, so their names are not included here.

In addition, I thank Diana Neff from Niwot United Methodist Church. She pulled a flatbed trailer to pick up the first *Maximum Saints Never Hide in the Dark* books. I admire her courage and commitment to help the incarcerated.

Thank you for all your hard work, prayers, support, assistance and encouragement. God bless you!

INTRODUCTION

Miracles Beyond Imagination

I grew up in Korea and have seen revival. After I came to the United States in 1979, I was missing something and I knew what it was – a revival. My definition of having a revival is to see many people being saved, many lives being transformed by God's love and power. Many people who gave their lives to serve God, and many who have the passion to save the lost.

If someone would have asked me what I wanted to see in America, it would be a revival. For a long time, I attended many different churches, and retreats in search of God, to experience revival. Many times, I sat and cried inside in worship services and retreats because I couldn't feel the presence of God. I asked, "Whenever I met people who are filled with joy and excitement, it's because they found Christ. Who has the passion for the lost souls? Would I ever be able to see a revival? God, where are you?" I kept asking these questions, but I received no answer.

I desperately wanted to see a revival, but I was only searching for it in other people. I was a luke-warm Christian and only following worldly desires and passion. Therefore, I had no desire to respond to the call of God when He called me into the ministry. Then God directed me to spend time in prayer, so I started praying for the revival of America. Soon, God had pointed out that the revival had to start in my heart first. Eventually, while I was writing a book, *Journey With Jesus*, God convinced me of the power of the Holy Spirit. That was the turning point in my life. I finally gave up my plans, and made a decision to go into the ministry to serve Jesus. This was the beginning of my own revival.

Before I started at The Iliff School of Theology, God spoke to me and I was called into prison ministry. Since then, God has opened many doors for me to minister to the incarcerated. I have been so blessed, and have seen many miracles.

I started working as a chaplain at the Adams County Detention Facility (ACDF) in December 2003. I learned that God can do much more than I could think, or imagine, if only I would follow the Holy Spirit's leading. The Holy Spirit planted the seed of revival in my heart, and my passion to see that kept growing. I just couldn't give up the vision of seeing a revival. For a long time, I lamented the fact that I didn't see revival taking place, and thought I would never see it. Interestingly, I have learned that many inmates at ACDF also were praying for a revival. I believe persistent prayer is the foundation of revival. I started a seven-week prayer project, with different themes, to promote revival. The first prayer project I started in 2004, was praying for "Revival and Healing of Our Souls."I encouraged the inmate leaders to remind others to pray for revival in their own pods.

I had led seven different prayer projects by the end of 2006. During that time, I started seeing something that I had never expected—a glimpse of revival. The Holy Spirit's presence in our facility was so powerful that we had many conversions and baptisms. Many were responding to the call to serve the Lord, and many plan to serve God when they are released. More than 500 people were baptized since I started working as a chaplain.

I give praise to our Lord Jesus, and the Holy Spirit for this wave of revival. I give thanks to Chaplain John Serio, who used to work with me, and who has touched many inmates in our facility. Also, Chaplain Rick who works with me now and is a dedicated powerful minister. In addition, I give thanks to all of the volunteers who are contributors to this revival. My next thanks goes to the Bible study, and prayer circle leaders in the pods. Without these leaders, there would be no revival! God let me see, hear, and feel this wave of revival through the inmate Christian leaders whom I call the "Maximum Saints." Maximum saints are not necessarily classified as maximum security inmates; I call them maximum saints because they are using their gifts to the maximum to serve the Lord. From time to time many Maximum Saints have preached sermons, and shared their testimonies of transformation, in Chaplain's Worship Services.

On February 2006, ten thousand copies of "Maximum Saints" stories were published in the book, *Maximum Saints Never Hide in the Dark*. This book was distributed in many other different jails and prisons: not only in Colorado but in other states with the support of many generous churches and individuals.

Many inmates in our facility have had transformation after reading *Maximum Saints*. Many chaplains, from different facilities, called me and said that *Maximum Saints* books helped many inmates in their facilities. The *Maximum Saints* book enlarged my vision to reach the incarcerated more than ever. At first, my plan was to produce only one book. But while I was working on the first book, God spoke to my heart that my vision was too small, and challenged me to work on more book projects. At ACDF, we have about 1,100 male and 200 female inmates. We are always short on inspirational books, and many other jails and prisons are in the same situation, or worse. Our facility has two full-time chaplains, but many other facilities do not even have a chaplain.

America has 2.3 million incarcerated; the largest prison population in the world. Just in Colorado, we have more than 20,000 prisoners in state prisons. When we count all of the detention facilities and Federal prisons, we have more than 30,000 incarcerated. Therefore, the ministry opportunity is wide open with this book ministry. Prior to the first distribution of *Maximum Saints*, I had been distributing my other books in jails and prisons. God enlarged my vision so that I was inspired to print ten thousand copies of *Journey With Jesus*, and with the support of many churches and friends, I have distributed them in many jails and prisons.

At the beginning of January of 2007, God was asking me to go back to my first seven-week prayer project so inmates can pray for the "Revival and Healing of Our Souls," so I did. By then, I developed "Jericho Prayer Walk," and "A Holy Fasting Prayer."I was able to encourage those who would like to participate in this prayer project and also to practice those prayers. Up until January 2007, I have seen the Holy Spirit's mighty power transform many lives, but I felt I was only seeing a glimpse of the revival. Then, in the middle of this prayer project in February, God helped me realize for the first time, that I was in the midst of a revival. I believe the book, *Maximum Saints*, is contributing to this revival. While I was working on the first *Maximum Saints* book, I felt like I was having a mountain top experience. I was filled with so much joy. I knew that this *Maximum Saints* book project was the work of the Holy Spirit. Then the second *Maximum Saints* book inspired me even more than the first one. "Thank you, Lord Jesus, for calling me to the prison ministry. Now, I don't have to have this longing for a revival. Thank you for helping me to realize that I am in the midst of a revival, and that you have blessed me through the maximum saints."

As a chaplain, I am privileged to meet many Maximum Saints, and hear their inspiring stories of transformation. But, most people on the outside (or inside the jail), only hear the horrible stories about the turmoil and violence in jail and prisons. It's true that violence and turmoil, can rule where many people are hurting, and going through so much suffering. This pain and suffering can be caused by many reasons: people's lack of understanding God's love and power of transformation; the lack of spiritual direction; and purpose in life without God. However, the *Maximum Saints* stories tell the world that God has not forgotten people who are hurting behind prison walls. God is blessing them by healing their hearts, lives, and helping them to forgive while giving direction in helping others who are going through turmoil.

From my own ministry experiences, Jesus manifests himself more behind jails, and prison walls, than any other ministry settings (like churches, homeless shelters, hospitals, nursing homes, retreats, mission fields, and Sunday schools). Why? The Bible explains why. Jesus said, *"It is not the healthy who need a doctor, but the sick. I have not come to call the righteous but the sinners to repentance."* (Luke 5:31-32) Many people behind prison walls desperately seek God. Many need spiritual healing and God brings healing. In the midst of pain and suffering, Maximum Saints are born; they raise other dead souls with the love and power of Christ.

Maximum Saints can create a powerful calming presence in the midst of a tumultuous, and violent environment. Many people have no idea how these Maximum Saints are saving other incarcerated people: from suicide to also stopping many violent situations by bringing peace. Christian messages create peace because God values people. When they are transformed by God's love, these people learn to value other people's lives. They start helping others instead of hurting themselves or others. Without these Maximum Saints, jails and prisons would be hell on earth.

Many Maximum Saints made a great impact on my spiritual growth, and these *Maximum Saints* books give a little glimpse of what I see and hear. Whenever I meet these saints, I know I have found God's treasure on Earth. I wish all of the outside people could see what I see. I wish everyone could hear what I hear. I wish the world could feel what I feel. I know it will be a grave sin for me not to share the stories of the *Maximum Saints* with others. James wrote, *"Anyone, then, who knows the good he ought to do and doesn't do it, sins."* (James 4:17)

Maximum Saints stories helped me to realize that God can bring the best out of each and everyone of us (even while incarcerated) because God's love and power brings healing and transforms people.

It's time to cheer for these forgotten, hidden, and unrecognized Maximum Saints! That is the reason for this book, *Maximum Saints*. God's love and healing power is spreading through the worst places like jails and prisons, because of these saints. Many Maximum saints have given all they have – their very lives – to go beyond their own pain to focus on caring for others who are wounded, and are in need of the healing presence of Jesus. In all circumstances, Jesus is worthy of our love and devotion. After all, Jesus is the only one who can bring salvation, joy, peace, hope, healing, and transformation in our hearts and lives. The Maximum Saints understand that.

Now, if anyone would ask me, "How can I experience a revival?" I would say, "Pray, but don't just pray. Praying is only the foundation for a revival. You will experience revival when you reach out to others who are hurting, especially the incarcerated and families of the incarcerated. I am saying this because what I couldn't find outside, I found it inside jail."

If you are a pastor in a church and want to see a revival, visit a jail or prison. I encourage you to start taking care of the spiritually sick and wounded people in jails and prisons. Remember, God called murderers like Moses, David, and Paul. When they responded to God's call and obeyed the Lord, God raised them to be our heroes! I encourage you to help your congregation to be involved in prison ministry by creating it in your own church, if you don't have one. Encourage every congregation to mentor the children of the incarcerated with the love of Christ.

Unless you are going to take care of the hurting people, you are not going to see a revival. You have to be in a place where Jesus shows himself to hurting people in order to see a revival. I have seen the Lord through many Maximum Saints and I am so grateful that God called me to prison ministry to share what God can do through these saints.

Chaplain Yong Hui McDonald

Part One:
Testimonials

"They overcame him by the blood of the lamb and by the word of their testimony." (Revelation 12:11a)

Drawing "Jesus on the Cross" by Charles Polk

1. I AM NO LONGER LOST — Gino Hinojosa

Looking back on my life of gangs, drugs, and crime, I remember that even from a very young age, Jesus was calling me. All of my life, whether I was in jail or out in the world, strangers would come up to me out of nowhere, tell me how Jesus loves me, and how He can save me. I just wasn't ready. I thought I was in control of my life. Boy, was I wrong. I had no control. I was a slave to sin! At age seven, I took my first hit of grass. At age nine, I had tasted my first drink of alcohol, and received my first tattoo. At age twelve, after being caught driving my motorcycle on the streets of Denver late one night, I was brought home by the police officer who stopped me. After searching me, he found me to be in possession of a straight razor, one ounce of grass, and an empty coke seal. He told my mom everything that he had found on me, and told her that I was headed for big trouble. Then, he put me in the back of the car. I thought I was going to jail, but instead he started telling me about Jesus and how He loved me. Of course I listened — anything to avoid jail.

At the age of sixteen, while most kids are learning how to play football, I had a needle in my arm, and experienced juvenile hall. I was in lockup without a clue where my life was headed. Coming from a poor, dysfunctional, broken home of five, in a rough east Denver neighborhood, I took to the streets, gangs, and drugs to escape the reality of being abused. I totally lost contact with who I was or why I was in this world. Little did I know I would spend the next twenty years battling the demons of addiction which left me spending all of my twenties and thirties in and out of prison; fifteen of those years were on the inside.

When all is said and done, I've always been tough — something I learned at a young age on the streets, and in juvenile hall. Going to church and talking about God was always a sign of weakness in my eyes. I sure didn't need God. I was tough with over two hundred pounds of attitude, and the capability for extreme violence. I knew it all and had seen it all;

guns and shootouts, knives and stabbings, needles and overdoses, smiles and cries.

I have lost so much over the years; wives, children, and all the material things this world has to offer. I had given up on ever being a normal, caring, and loving man. I figured I would end up dead, or in prison for the rest of my life. I was hopeless and didn't even know it. I knew I was lost; I just didn't know how to get to normal.

On April 27, 2005, I had been given parole and another chance to get it right. I met the most beautiful woman, and fell in love. I started subcontracting electrical jobs. I had my children and family in my life with their love and full support. But, I was doing it Gino's way; I had forgotten that was always the wrong way! I thought that all I had wasn't enough. I wanted more women, more money, and more of this big pie that I felt was owed to me. Once again, I started using drugs and losing me. When I looked up, everything I had gained was lost.

On November 5, 2005, I was charged with attempted murder. I was sent to jail. I was kicking drugs. I lost my girl, my children, my life, my home, my business, and my car. I was in a cell again, knew I would never get out of prison again and if I did I would be too old to care. My life had just ended. I had hit rock bottom so many times before, that I knew what it felt like, and even had a system for dealing with it. This time, it would be different, and more intense than I ever could imagine.

I had broken down once again, and there was no coming out of this one! I found myself unable to stop crying. The pain of what was going on was a hundred times worse than I remembered. I was in total despair: hopeless, lost, and in such pain that all I could do was cry myself to sleep. I would eat, go back to my cell, crawl under the desk or bed, and wail at the top of my lungs, pleading with God, "GOD, PLEASE HELP ME! O GOD, PLEASE HELP ME!" The guards and my cellie thought I was dying. I thought I was already dead. Then I fell into a deep sleep, and God came to me. In my dream, I was on my knees in some dirt in a place I had never been before. I was crying, and I felt what I thought was rain on my head. I looked up, and right in front of me was Jesus on the Cross. He was crying, and the blood from His hand was dripping on my head. He looked down at me with tears in His eyes. He said my life was wrong in God's eyes. He told me to repent and change from my ways. He said He loved me — to take His hand, and follow Him. If not, He would come when I least expected it, and I would not be ready. He said to choose. I chalked all this up to hallucinations from kicking drugs. I had these dreams every time I went to sleep for three days straight.

On the third day, in a cold cell, I surrendered my life to Jesus. I haven't been the same since. I have been delivered from being a slave to Satan. The last offer from the District Attorney was for twenty to thirty-two years if I would plead out to first degree assault with a deadly weapon while on parole. I went to trial. I was found guilty of second degree assault in a crime of passion which carries one to three years. Jesus has truly saved me! I wasn't supposed to walk out of here this time. Now I am saved. Jesus has been there all along for me! All I had to do was turn to Him, lean on Him, trust in Him, and believe in Him.

I look back on all the times strangers and people I would run across would tell me about Jesus and God. One time in 1992, I was working for MCI calling people from state to state to ask whether they would like to change to MCI from AT&T. I was hooked on coke and heroin at the time. I called a family in California, and the guy at the other end told me how he only allowed one phone in his home because he was a Christian, and one was all he needed. He told me how he had been hooked on heroin, spent 10 years in prison, gave his life to Jesus, had been clean for 10 years, and how he now has a great life. This guy didn't know me, and yet he told me that he knew that I had called him for a reason. He asked if we could pray over the phone. I didn't want to disrespect him, so I agreed. He prayed that Jesus would come to me and open my eyes. He knew something was wrong and asked me what was going on. I told him that I couldn't say, and he told me the only way out was

Jesus.

Fifteen years later, I look back, and I see how right he was. How lost I was. How Jesus has saved me from death so many times. I'm so thankful to be alive and healthy. My number one priority in life is to find out what God's will is for me. I can't be free, I can't be a father, I can't be a husband, and I can't be a member of society without God. I am a nobody who wants to tell everybody about somebody who can save anybody! I should have listened long before, but I was too hard-headed and my heart was hardened. God Himself had to come to me so I would surrender to His plan for my life. He has saved me, cleansed me, and now I am a new man in Christ!

It's really something to see the absolute joy on the faces of people who knew me before when they see what God has done to me. They don't even recognize me. The pain, shame, guilt, hatred, and anger are gone. I've been delivered from drug addiction, alcoholism, and sin. We all still struggle with sin, but being saved gives us the strength through Jesus to overcome sin. We are victorious in Jesus and His blood on the cross at Calvary. I've been freed after thirty years of being a slave to sin. Now, I'm a bond servant to Jesus Christ. Now I am free! I've totally surrendered my life to the will of God.

I witness to everyone who will listen. I love to serve God. I keep it real. I'm a Christian in the pod, in the yard, in my cell, and in the shower! I stay in the Word of God, praying diligently. I have fallen in love with Jesus because He came to me, saving me, loving me, and caring for me when I didn't even love myself. It's tough sometimes. It's not easy picking up my cross daily and following Jesus. It's an on-going process, not an event! I know I can trust in God's love and plan for me. I'm no longer lost! Praise God!

2. MY TESTIMONY — Michah Collins

I want to share with you how God has used me, not only in the Adams County Jail, but also in many other institutions in the State of Colorado. But first, I'd like to tell you a bit about my background.

I was born in Fort Scott, Kansas, a small country town, on August 22, 1974. When I was seven years old, my father was murdered. He became my mother's deceased husband, and I became a fatherless child. Upon losing her husband, my mother fled to Colorado to escape the horror and memory of such a tragedy.

My father's death had a powerful impact on me. At eleven years of age, while searching for a father figure, I was led into drugs and gang violence. I have a very dark past and was in and out of group homes. At the age of fourteen, I was charged as an adult in bad company and became the youngest person in the state of Colorado to serve time in the Department of Corrections.

I can remember crying, and looking out my prison window when I was sixteen; wondering what all the other sixteen year olds in the world were doing. I had to fight for my life, being the youngest inmate out of a thousand men in Canyon City, and I experienced some horrible things behind those prison bars.

I began to hear God's call and got saved in prison at seventeen years of age. After that, although I continued to be in and out of prison, God chose to use me in a mighty way. Eventually, I came to the Adams County jail where I was classified as a maximum security inmates on January 3, 2005. At that time, the maximum inmates didn't get to have church. I prayed that we would eventually be allowed to have church. God's response was, "That's what I have you here for." I began to lead a Bible study in our pod and watched men's lives changed by the power of God.

After three months, I bonded out, but after a year's time, I lost at trial and was returned to the Adams County Jail. But, here's the miracle: I came back to the same pod, the same cell, and the same bed, only to see that God was still moving in B Module, Pod 3. Other maximum saints were praying and doing the work of God in my absence. As I watched men's lives being changed, a young man named Jason Vigil moved into my cell. I heard God's voice say, "He's one of mine, and there is work to be done." As our relationship began to grow, I was able to minister to him. He mentioned his girlfriend, Marla Rose, who lost her life from an overdose. He wondered if she had made it to heaven.

One day, when the book, *Maximum Saints Never Hide in the Dark*, came to us, I opened it up to a page that said, "A Friend Named Marla." Right away I heard Jason's name in my mind, so I took the book to him and said, "Read this." Minutes later, he came to me, crying. Lo and behold, it was the story of Marla Rose. Another maximum saint had introduced Marla to Jesus, and she had given her life to God. Though Marla lost her life, she also was released from jail and is now free. I tell this story so that you might look at the awesome power of God. After all, when Jason knew where his Marla is resting, he began to ask me questions about God. And now, he's another one who has been won for the kingdom.

3. GOD OPENED MY HEART — Chastity Suazo

I have battled with addiction my whole life. Ever since I was fourteen years old, I've been locked up in some kind of facility: juvenile, rehab, foster homes, jail, halfway houses, and eventually - prison. I am twenty-four years old and am here at ACDF on a parole violation, thank God. Jesus must really love this knucklehead because he never lets me stray too far. Thank you Jesus! In the time I've been here at ACDF, I have felt, seen, and heard Jesus' Holy Spirit work within me like I've never seen, heard or felt before.

Writing this brings tears to my eyes because never would I have thought that the hate and anger inside of me over my brother's death would diminish like it has. May 18th, four years ago, my brother was murdered. He was shot in the back twice by a man I didn't know. We lived in Grand Junction, a town where everybody knew everybody. Kris was twenty-three years old—very young.

My brother was my protector and my security. When things got rough, he was there. When I was eighteen years old, we lost my father. Kris was twenty at the time. My dad was my brother's hero. When my father died, my brother and I went on self-destructive missions. I'm sure all of you out there can relate in some form or another. Drugs played a part, a huge part, in letting the devil control the path that I would choose to take in life.

My brother died in the ambulance shortly after he was shot. I have held hate, resentment, and anger in my heart ever since that early morning that my mother came to the halfway house to tell me my brother was gone. I came face to face with my brother's murderer about two months later. I called him every degrading name I could think of, spit in his face, and put my hands on him. He got off on self defense. My family was baffled, to say the least. Time has gone on, as it inevitably does.

December 17, 2006, I was baptized in the name of the Father, and of the Son, and of the Holy Spirit — thank you Jesus! That wasn't the only great thing that happened that Sunday. We were sitting in church, and during prayer, the chaplain asked us to sit, and just listen to the Holy Spirit. Listen...I asked the Holy Spirit to tell me what I should pray for. A few minutes passed by, and then it hit me.

Plain as day, He told me that I needed to forgive the guy who killed my brother. I felt overwhelmed! Tears started coming! I got down on my knees, and started praying for him and his family; telling God that I forgive him, that I love him, and that if it is in God's will, to please give me the opportunity to someday come face to face with this man. I want to tell him that I love him, that I forgive him, and that he needs to forgive himself. I don't harbor any negative feelings toward him, or his family. I also prayed that the guilt and shame he carries would be taken away, because God forgives him. From my heart, mind, and soul, I forgive him also.

You see, God opened my heart so much that I was able to forgive this man. God is good all the time. He is always on time. The overwhelming feeling of love I felt at that moment, could only have come from the Holy Spirit. Thank you Jesus!

4. GOD HAVE MERCY ON YOUR SOUL – Steven Rodriguez

I am a new believer in the Lord Jesus Christ. I found Jesus at a very painful point in my life when I finally had exhausted every other means to find the truth about life. I completely surrendered my life to Jesus on March 11, 2006, in the segregation unit of the ACDF, following a suggestion from my dad.

Since making that choice, I have been trying really hard to be obedient to the Lord, and His direction. I pray every day, and I spend hours every day studying the Bible. I'm in the sixteenth course of the Set Free Correspondence Emmaus Bible Studies, and I feel like my life is moving in a better direction than it ever has before. It's a process that will take a lifetime to complete, but I am finally finding peace in my heart, free from the weight of pain that my first thirty-two years of life have brought me. The healing has begun and continues. "Thank you, Jesus, for saving a wretch like me," are words I will spend a lifetime saying, and still never be able to say them enough. My life has changed drastically!

When I was in prison seven years ago, I met a guy from the other side of the world. Both sides were in squalor and evil. I was a thug from Commerce City—angry, bitter, and hate-filled. Mike was a white supremacist from New Jersey and had a dark side to him that even made me cringe at times. Our paths crossed because of music. We both could play different instruments, and we both had a passion for dark, heavy music. Mike and I got a few other guys and formed a heavy metal band.

Over a two year time span, we spent countless hours practicing and writing our own music. We both had a demented way of expressing ourselves through our songs through both the hardcore crunch and vicious lyrics. He once told me that I was one of his very few friends; an honor I accepted because Mike hated everybody. He didn't like anybody, and I rarely did myself.

The other morning I was in line to take my morning meds, and I ran into another guy I knew from back then. We were talking, and he asked me if I'd heard about what happened to Mike. I told him, "No, what?"

My friend Mike had spent close to thirty years inside prison walls. Then finally he got a chance and was released. I didn't even get a chance to be happy for Mike, because the story wasn't finished. For some reason only God and Mike know: Mike hung himself in his sister's garage.

Throughout my life, I've known a lot of people that died. I've always been one to accept death as part of human existence. But hearing about Mike hurt me the most. The reason is this: He just might be the first person I've known that in all likelihood won't be in heaven when I get there. I grieve deep in my heart at the thought.

I pray that God softened Mike's heart and sent one of His saints to tell my friend about Jesus. I pray that my friend accepted Jesus as his personal Savior, and was born again, before he left this world. I do not want to let one unsaved person die and be condemned to hell for all eternity. Peter tells us that the Lord is not wanting anyone to perish. (2 Peter 3:9) That means that even dark people, like my friend Mike, is in the heart of God, our mighty Creator. I thank God for His love and grace. He saved me, I know; but I feel a sense of urgency for all the people who are unsaved. Having a person I personally knew and cared about possibly die in a lost condition is an experience I never want again. "I surrender to you, Father in heaven, take me and use me to save the unsaved. Bless me with a boldness to be a witness for my Lord Jesus."

I say now is the time to give up the resistance! The time is short, and our next breath in this life isn't guaranteed. When this life is over, our chance for salvation is over, too! Everything that is given to us is an opportunity to share what Jesus did for us. We have to do it! Souls in eternity may very well depend on our obedience. Yes, obedience does include reaching out to the unsaved, the unloved, the lost and introducing them to our best friend, our Savior, our God. This is important, and a commandment of the Lord Jesus himself. *Acts 10:42 says, "He commanded us to preach to the people and to testify that he is the one whom God appointed as judge of the living and the dead."*

Being a child of God: a co-heir, being in Jesus, we are called to spread the good news to everybody. Pray for opportunities to tell of the love God has for us, shown by sending His only begotten Son, to pay the price for our sins. *(John 3:16)* Have any of us ever truly wished anybody to hell? I have not, and it's my sincere hope that nobody else has either. We have to take the initiative in turning others away from hell. We do that by completely surrendering every aspect of our existence to the work of God: seeking His wisdom, and scriptural understanding while being equipped with proper Bible doctrine. Be ready at all times to tell of the blessings God has given you. Pray for the unsaved. Pray that all hearts will be touched, opened, and ready to accept the gift of life that is given to us through our Lord Jesus. Let yourself be a tool that the Lord uses to reach out to unbelievers.

"Mike, I hope somebody was able to reach you before you left. You have lit a fire in my heart to do all I can, with God's help, to save any unbeliever I meet. I pray that God may have mercy on your soul. I will never forget you, and I'll miss you. I am your friend, your brother in Christ."

5. A TRUE STORY OF REVIVAL — Jose Marquez

When I was on the streets, I dedicated myself to selling drugs, and also to doing other illegal things. I went to church one time, and I answered an altar call. There I accepted Christ. But truly, at that time I didn't know what was going on. I was still the same person. I kept on drinking, using drugs, and even cheating on my wife.

One day, I found out that my wife was cheating on me. I stayed at home to confront her, but she never came home. A voice inside my head was telling me to leave, but I didn't listen. I was so mad that I wouldn't leave. I wanted to know what was going on. At that moment, the police came to arrest me. My wife had called the cops on me, and I ended up in custody at ACDF.

In here, I had problems with an inmate, but we resolved it. Then, one day, I was listening to Spanish music on my headphones and I heard my wife dedicating a song to her lover. I became extremely depressed, and I tried to commit suicide. I tore a sheet and wrapped it as tightly as I could around my neck. My cellmate told the deputy. I ended up in medical housing on suicide watch for a week. In medical, I didn't eat anything, and I also had problems with an inmate there.

Five days into medical treatment, I was in bed. I heard a positive voice in my head that all this was happening for a reason. I thought about my children and doing something positive for my children. In the holding tank, when I went to court, I had a problem with an inmate. He choked me and I fainted. Then, he slammed me on the ground, split my head open, and I ended up in the hospital. After release from the hospital, I ended up in Module A-1, and a brother in Christ started sharing with me the gospel of salvation. I still didn't feel secure about myself. I still thought that my life had no meaning and that not even God could help me. I went to the hole, and I read the book, *A Divine Revelation of Hell*, by Mary Baxter. It was then that I finally came to my senses, both spiritually and mentally.

After I got out of the hole, I kept on going to the Bible studies that brother Omar was having throughout the week. I accepted Jesus as my Lord and Savior. From that point on, I started developing a relationship with God. I started doing my own Bible studies through the mail. *John 3:16* had a great impact on me and *Galatians 4:4-6* helped me. Paul said, *"For through the law I died to the law so that I might live for God. I have been crucified with Christ and I no longer live, but Christ lives in me. The life I live in the body, I live by faith in the Son of God, who loved me and gave himself for me." (Galatians 2:19-20)*

Even though I am a prisoner, God has adopted me as His son through His grace. Now, that my faith grows, I have joy, peace, and serenity that I have found nowhere else. Serving God is not easy. It is hard. But as Paul said, *"Whatever you have learned or received or heard from me, or seen in me – put it into practice. And the God of peace will be with you." (Philippians 4:9)* Now I understand that why I suffered all of this, is so that I would find God, so I would not perish, but have everlasting life.

6. GOD IS TRAINING ME — Connie Russom

When you are locked up, your true self screams out to you. At that time, you either pay attention or ignore the screaming and pay the consequences. Being at Adams County Jail has helped me to see so much that I overlooked. My past led me into a disappointment that I never want to feel again; not only disappointment, but also loss. Most of all, failure to myself and family.

I had been in disciplinary for four days starting Dec. 6, 2006. During that time, I had court on Thursday, and I expected to go home. My Pre Sort Investigation (PSI) recommended the female offender program (FOP). The District Attorney (DA) had no argument, but the judge thought that since I had been on probation for two years for a felony 3 - schedule 2 charges, and had failed to comply, he would give me a five year sentence at community corrections; with also two years on the felony 6, that violated my probation.

I returned back to disciplinary, and was very upset. When I was escorted to my cell, I was easily angered by the deputy slamming the door. My misbehavior sent me to the quiet cell, which is located in the booking area. I wasn't in a place I wanted to be after court. I wanted to hear that I was going home! I sat and cried in the hole for the next two days. I stopped reading my Bible. I had convinced my self that God wasn't real. I was let out of the hole at 11:30 a.m. and was placed in the maximum pod. I didn't want to be "maxed out," as it is referred to in jail. When the deputy came in, I was told to change out of my red suit and get into orange and white. I did, and "chow"(breakfast) had come. I ate and drank a cup of coffee. Lockdown was called, and I tried to sleep.

I had made a daily routine schedule, and in that schedule, I had written "Bible study." I began reading the book of Isaiah, and verse nine was highlighted. So that's the first thing I read that morning when I thought I first felt the Lord. I worked out after a while, and then the chaplain came. She made an announcement that she was going to cancel worship because it was close to dinner time, but she decided to do a short service for maximum inmates.

My awakening came when I sat in front of the chaplain in that short service. She led a prayer and then gave a sermon about how to find peace. In one of the illustrations of her sermon, she talked about a man who went to court and was devastated. He stopped praying because he was upset with the sentence. When she described what happened to the man, she was describing everything I had been through in the last couple of days. Then she ended in saying that the Lord did this because there's something else He wants to teach us.

I have been in ACDF for three months. Since December 7, 2006, I have been fighting my old demons, but not by myself. Out of two hundred female inmates, why did the chaplain hit it right on the nose with my situation? After I spoke to the chaplain, and told her about the way she really woke me up, with a slap in the face back to reality, I gave my heart to the One and only, Lord God. I have also committed myself to His Word. I am faithfully reading His Word, but taking it one day at a time. I have been real with Him (and myself) that I have become a woman who wants to change her life around.

I am not the type of person who preaches, but I want everyone to know that our Lord is real and He is good. I have always been the type of person who does not say things but just does things. "Don't say it, be about it." Now that I am on the road to change, I finally see a future for me: a successful one, to boot. I am no longer feeling the shame and guilt of my past. I have had it all, and now, I see that none of this lasted. No one is helping me or caring for me in here. I now feel loved because I love myself. I feel confident going to the halfway house program and completing it.

I have learned that to heal yourself, you must go through suffering, and you should not just make promises. Before I was incarcerated, I also suffered. Let me tell you, those streets are nothing nice. I have walked alone on the dark road with the monkey on my back. But now, I realize that my Father God wants to lead me in the light, and hold my hand whether the road is smooth or rough. The only One I truly believe in with all my heart and soul, died on the Cross so I can be forgiven. He is the Almighty God: who hovers above and hears my every cry. I will be released from my chains, and I will become a new creature of God.

7. THE LORD GIVES US CROSSROADS — Cordell Stephens

On May 5, 2006, I went to court thinking I would be there in time to call my son and spend some time with him. I told myself, "The judge will give me more time to pay the restitution." As I boarded the bus, I even thought of what truths (and half truths) I would say to get out of it. I arrived at 9:45 a.m., but by 11:00 a.m., I was in the holding cell of the courtroom, trying to figure out what I would do for the next six months. That was my sentence because I chose not to pay restitution. Instead, I fed my needs: drugs, weed, and things I really didn't need.

While sitting there I thought to myself, "Why would God do this to me?" It took some time for me to see that He was not punishing me, but He was blessing me. Some of you may ask how God could be blessing me by putting me in jail. It was one of the many questions that I had to ask myself, especially while I was in Intake. I knew why I was in jail, but why me? Why now? It took about two weeks for me to see and understand why.

As a child I was baptized and saved. I knew the Lord: I was a junior layman, and I was a lamb in His flock. But as I grew older, I strayed away from that flock. My mother and father had always told me that I needed to go to church with Jesus. Over the years, and especially the last two years, I would only pray when my family needed to pray. I thought those prayers were in vain. Nothing went right. I couldn't hold a job, or keep my son out of a foster home. I also didn't have any type of meaningful relationships. I was a mess and I knew it. I knew what I needed to do, but I didn't do it. Then, the Lord blessed me by putting me in jail.

Once I was housed in F2200, the cloudy haze of indecision started to leave my system. My thoughts were clear, but they seemed to be occupied with the fact that I was in jail. What would I do with my time? I didn't know anyone in here, and I didn't have any friends to call. Then, a young man named Lloyd spoke to me, and he made me feel okay. We talked for a minute but not much more. Later that night, he met with five or six others at a table. My curiosity was peaked. As I approached the table, I could hear the words they were saying. They brought back memories — memories of a childhood long ago — Wednesday's night prayer meeting.

As I sat down, they welcomed me, and one shared his Bible so that I could follow along. As the discussion continued, I remained quiet. As I listened, I started to realize why I was here. I had strayed too far from the flock. The Lord wanted me back amongst his sheep. *Psalms 23:1* says, *"The Lord is my shepherd, I shall not be in want."* Before my blessing, I wanted too much and didn't believe that God would provide. I did other things to provide for myself. If I had had a deeper faith, I would have been blessed with what I needed.

At times, the Lord gives us decisions to make: crossroads, if you will. Because we have free will, those decisions are reflections of our faith. My faith was so little in God and so deep in worldly things, that the Lord needed to wake me up with this blessing, the blessing of going to jail! Coming to jail has given me time to dry out and focus. Once my system was clear, I was able to focus on my faith. As the last few weeks have gone by, I have realized that no matter how lonely I felt, God is always with me. I began to see the abundant blessings in front of me. I could be laid up in a hospital: I could be homeless, and in the ghetto; I could be on the run from the law, doing way too much of the devil's work. Instead, I am regaining my faith in God.

I have all the time I need to meditate, pray, and read the Word of God. My mind is open to receive the blessings of His Word and to apply His teachings to my life. I am able to spread the Word of God because I am blessed. I say to those who hear or read this, "Do not think that being in jail is something bad. Look at it as God telling you and me that we were doing too much: that we need to stand down so we may be able to receive Him and His blessings. Then, so we can free our minds to think and see clearly."

I challenge each and every one of you to think outside the devil's box. Look at where you are and ask, "Am I blessed?" If you are alive, you are blessed. If you have your mind, can make a choice, then you are blessed. Allow yourself the chance for salvation. Allow God to come into your life or allow him back in. Don't wait until a blessing (like coming to jail) happens to you, to open your eyes to the great things that God can do. I can honestly say that my eyes have been opened, and I am truly blessed.

8. TWICE FALLEN — Cody Tapia

I was sentenced on May 3, 2005, to eight years in Community Corrections. Prior to my sentencing, I spent eleven months in ACDF fighting my case. When I was first incarcerated, I was a lost soul. I had always loved Jesus but had never truly given myself to our Lord. Like others, I believe in my heart that our Lord Jesus placed me in these situations to save my soul. I was on a path of destruction. Not only was I killing myself with drugs, I was also making my family suffer. I hated doing this, but I wasn't strong enough to stay away from the lure of drugs. Ultimately, this landed me in jail for the first time in my life. I firmly believe that our Lord did this for me because I wasn't strong enough to stop the destruction in my life.

Those eleven months in this jail truly saved my life in more ways than one. When I called out to our Lord Jesus for help, He saved me. I felt the best I've ever felt in my life and I was in jail. With the teachings of the Holy Spirit, I had prepared myself spiritually to go back into society a changed person.

I went to the Phoenix Center prepared. As in 1 *Peter 1:13 -16*, *"Therefore, prepare your minds for action; be self-controlled; set your hope fully on the grace to be given you when Jesus Christ is revealed. As obedient children, do not conform to the evil desires you had when you lived in ignorance. But just as He who called you is holy, so be holy in all you do; for it is written: 'Be holy, because I am holy.'"*

My first week at the halfway house was one of the best weeks of my life. I was blessed with two jobs within the first week. I soon found out that having two jobs kept me so occupied that I had no time for trouble. I worked so hard and I made client of the month twice while there. My plan was going perfectly. After nine months at the halfway house, I was granted non-residence, and moved in with my father. This program also kept me real busy with daily breath tests, drug tests twice a month and many classes that were required. I was another step closer to getting my life back together. During all these times, I was doing everything I thought I needed to do to succeed.

If you haven't already noticed from my testimony, during this time, I made the worst mistake I could have made. I lost my walk with our Lord Jesus. I turned my back on our Lord when the times were good. I fell right back into the devil's trap. The sad part about it was that I knew that I was turning my back on our Lord. While in jail, I was so in tune with the Lord, the Bible, and the Holy Spirit, that I knew what I needed was Jesus in my life. I didn't stick with what I knew would save me, our Lord Jesus. I thought I could do it on my own.

After being in the non-residence program for two months, I started to get more freedom. This is where the devil was waiting for me with open arms. Slowly, I started to hang out with the same friends I had before I was arrested. I resisted the temptations for a short time, but it was only a matter of time until I thought I could get away with using meth just a couple of times. I thought to myself, "I'm different now and I can handle it just a couple of times."

As some of you already know, it never works that way! After two more months of fooling myself and fooling the system by covering up my urinalyses in various ways, I finally was caught. On May 20, 2006, while I was meeting with my counselor, my car was searched. About a gram of meth was found. Needless to say, I was regressed and charged with another felony.

The sad part about it, was that I knew something bad was going to happen. I had turned my back on the only person who could truly keep me out of trouble—Jesus! The devil used another one of his tools to keep me down—guilt! I never knew guilt could be such a strong feeling. I felt guilty because I had let down everyone. It was so hard to have to tell everyone that I had failed again. To tell you the truth, it still hurts me, but I'm not going to let the devil bring me down. I'm not going to let the devil keep me away from our Lord Jesus. I know the Lord loves me too much to let me fall. Sometimes we fail to understand why these things happen to us in our lives. I know that this is happening for a reason. I simply have to surrender myself to our Lord Jesus, and let Him carry me through these hard times.

I see now that I can't do things my own way. I see now that I need the Lord as the Leader of my life. While surrendering to Jesus, I must try to learn what I did wrong, and try again to do things right. I'm seeing now that Jesus is teaching me to become a stronger person; this is His plan, not mine! I'm going to surrender myself by prayer, reading the Bible, and asking our Lord to have His Holy Spirit lead my life. I would like to share a Scripture that has helped me so much through these hard times. I pray that my testimony as well as 1 Peter 1:3-7 may help you if you also have fallen.

9. I AM NO LONGER ON THE WRONG PATH — S.A.

I was just 14 years old: a normal kid who went to school and got good grades and I felt good about myself. I was a freshman in high school. I had never even thought of being in gangs or using any type of drugs. Much less, being locked up in jail. All of this changed at the end of that year. I started hanging out with older, more vicious kids who smoked and drank. I remember always telling my mom I would never use drugs or be in gangs. All of this changed when I started down the wrong path.

One day, this guy who was new in school convinced me to join the gang he was in, so I did. He told me how cool it was to be a gang member. I went down the drain from there. I stopped going to school, started causing trouble, tagging walls, and fighting. Somehow, I passed my sophomore year. I thought I was invincible: that nothing could happen to me, as long as I had my homeboys. That summer, I really fell into sin: I started doing cocaine. At first it was just a bump, but in a few months, I was doing it almost every day, especially at parties. I thought I was "cool" doing all these drugs.

By the time I was in the eleventh grade, I almost never went to school, and one day I got kicked out. That's when it really got bad. I stopped caring about life itself. All I knew was that I was in a gang and I had to be down for it in order to gain some respect. I tried to be the "baddest" I could be. But, every time I did something bad, I would realize that it was bad and wrong, but I did it anyway.

Drugs and alcohol took over my mind and my life. That's all I wanted to do. I would spend the money I had worked for all week on drugs and alcohol. My mom tried to stop me, but I wouldn't listen. I didn't care about anything but the gang and the drugs. I remember the "homeboys" telling me to do this or that, and I would do it just so they would think I was bad. I don't know what happened to me. I had never been in this type of life as I was growing up. It only took two years for me to end up in jail.

One night, I was getting drunk and high: the rest, I cannot say. Two days later, I was at the juvenile facility charged with accomplice to attempted murder. That day, it all hit me. I realized how ignorant I had been for two years. I had wasted my time fighting and doing things for some people who said they were my friends. Now that I am here, I have found God. I had never realized how gracious God is. I started reading the Bible, and it has opened my eyes to a whole new beginning.

Now I sit in my cell praying for forgiveness: praying for everything to go right. I feel closer to God than ever before, and I thank God every day for opening my eyes and giving me a chance to turn my life around and follow His path, the path where being a good person has its price but also has the reward of realizing that life is full of opportunities. I thank God for rescuing me from the path of sins and now pray for my life to be full of love for other people and for myself. I don't know how long I am going to be in jail, but I know that God will always be with me to guide me on the way to His kingdom in the heavens above.

10. LET YOUR TEARS WRITE — Cecilia Medina

I went to the chaplain's worship three weeks ago; she encouraged me to write my testimony. She told me to let my tears write it, but to focus on forgiveness. After my first try, I sat in my cell for two weeks looking over what I had written, and saw it was nothing but blame; I blamed the men in my life who were all women beaters. My first almost succeeded in making it impossible for me to conceive. (The Lord had other plans and blessed me with four sons—my miracles and my angels!) There were always men full of anger and jealousy in my life. Not knowing how to love myself, most of the time I was looking for love in all the wrong places. Maybe I was even seeking a father-figure, someone who would love me, cherish the tender moments we shared, and have a love so strong it would be unconditional. If so, I didn't find him. I would wake up one more time bruised and battered, and with my heart shattered.

February sixth of this year, I walked into my house and found my first-born dead on the floor just weeks before his twenty-first birthday. He had died from hypothermia. I was sure it was my man's fault. I lost everything at once: my son, my man, and my house, just like that. I slept on porches and in parks, and even went all the way to Utah to live with my husband and his girlfriends. I knew I would probably drink myself to death if I were alone. After three weeks in Utah, I came back home more traumatized than before I left.

I started throwing myself into work, and became a certified flagger. I'd only have a beer or two on Saturdays. There was no way I was going to be standing in the sun eight to ten hours, Monday through Friday, with a hangover.

From the autopsy report, I found out that my man had nothing to do with killing my son, just as everyone had said. I asked him to forgive me for not having faith. But here I sit, two months later, and he hasn't even tried to help me. He ran away again! But Jesus never did. I accepted Jesus into my heart September 13, and He showed me how to forgive. Through His word He forgave me! Finally, I have that cherished, unconditional love I've been looking for all this time. My son once said to me, "You don't need any man, Mom, you got me!" Well, it's like that with Jesus. I feel like that is what He is saying to me. My son's name is Angelo, and he's waiting for me with the Lord in Heaven. And all those men? I forgave them and put them in God's hands. The Lord has bigger and better plans for me. Amen!

11. THE LORD BEGAN TO SPEAK TO ME — Hope

What do you do when God puts you in a place where all you can do is focus on His glory and His purpose? You pray. You fall to your knees, and beg for forgiveness. After that, you ask for direction. Since I've gotten here, I've been praying to the Lord. I have pleaded with the Almighty for forgiveness, and then I asked God to allow His will to be done. No matter what the outcome is, I want His purpose to be filled. I begin to pray for direction, and I have prayed for God to open my heart: that I might receive Him more, and that I might be able to discern good from evil. Next, I pray for my faith and guidance. After that, it's for obedience. After that, something else, and then something else. I pray day and night.

Sometimes, I become frustrated with God. I begin to accept the spirit of doubt from the devil. Other times I would feel that my prayers were in vain: that the Lord had abandoned me; and that I was so far gone to the world that I'd be lost forever. I was in real "Big trouble." So, I decided to give it one more try. I fell to my knees and told the Lord, "Okay, enough is enough." I began to completely surrender myself to the Lord. I gave myself over to Him. My way of talking, my way of thinking, my way of moving, the things that I thought I "loved" — I gave all over to God. It was a humbling experience. I don't think I've cried so much in a long time.

After my total surrender, I went back and prayed to the Lord again. I questioned Him, "Why do I come to you and talk to you if you will not answer me?" I begged the Lord to let me hear His voice. That night, before I went to bed, I read *Journey of Mystical Spiritual Experiences* by Chaplain McDonald. In the book, it said to be quiet and wait. That was my answer. I spent so much time throwing prayers into the air, one right after the other that I never had a moment of quiet meditation. I never gave God a chance to answer me.

The next time I fell to my knees, I said, "Lord, give me your Holy Word. Speak to my heart." I still had requests, but this time the Spirit said, "Hush." I was quiet, but there was nothing, so I stayed there on my knees a little longer - still quiet. Then, it happened. The Lord began to speak to me. I am sure you can imagine the shock: better yet, the joy I felt. I asked the Lord, "Why didn't you speak to me before?" He said, "My child, you never gave me the chance." I asked Him, "What am I supposed to do with what You've called me to do?" The Lord said, "Nothing, I need you to first become stronger in Christ. Then, my child, I will do the rest." I asked, "How do I become strong in Christ?" The Lord said, "Through my spoken word child. It is in the Gospel. Read it. Memorize its scriptures and share my saving grace with others."

After that night, I began to have many conversations with the Lord. I began to fully open up and develop a truly personal relationship with my Father, a relationship built on open two-way communication.

Sometimes, when we speak to the Father, we don't know what He does with our prayers and it can be quite discouraging. We can feel far away from Him. We can feel like the Lord is giving us the silent treatment. But, if we can learn to be quiet, and wait on the Lord, we will find that He has been waiting for the opportunity to speak to our hearts. All it takes is to give up control. To allow God into the driver's seat of our lives for total surrender to His good and perfect will for us. Then, the Lord can guide us and communicate with us freely without our interrupting Him. Through love, obedience, and patiently waiting on the Lord, we open our hearts to have a truly personal relationship with our wise and ever-loving Father.

12. I HEARD THE MOST CALMING, GENTLE VOICE
— Kristine Madril

Because of having some pretty major stuff going on in my life, I put my faith in Christ briefly at thirteen years of age. By the age of sixteen, I started to shoot heroin. I was extremely addicted, out of control, on the streets. To top it all off, from the age of six, I had been influenced by people in a pagan religion.

By the age of nineteen, I was a full blown Satan worshipper and strung out on coke and heroin.

On February 23, 2000, I overdosed on meth. Somewhere along the line, I slammed a mix of three drugs, which finished me off! My dad was also strung out, and he did not know what to do. He called my sister and told her I was dying upstairs. I was gone, and I went to hell. I saw dark, cold and empty looking demons. One of them had his hand out to me. As I was about to give him my hand, I heard the most calming, gentle man's voice. It was just beautiful, and all he said was, "Make your choice." I pulled my hand back and turned around with my eyes closed. I put my arms up, and said, "Please, don't leave me." Everything went calm. My soul felt weird, but comforted.

This all happened at the point where my family was with me and the priest was reading the Sacrament of the Sick. I remember feeling almost mad at them. I wanted them to know I was okay; that God had me. After three weeks on life support, I woke up and started a brand new life with God. I relearned how to do everything; read, write, et cetera.

13. I WILL NEVER LEAVE YOU NOR FORSAKE YOU
— Jess Montez

It all started on the streets of San Antonio, Texas, in 1966. I was jumped into the West Side Gang, and there was no turning back. It seemed like nothing to me at the time. It was easy stealing cars, and stripping them for parts to make money, burglaries, and breaking into boxcars. We were making lots of money, or so it seemed at the time. With drug use always comes dealing drugs until you get strung out, and armed robbery becomes your game. It is real hard game trying to keep in step with the "fast game," or ahead of it. I got caught up in a murder case at fourteen years old.

It took about a year for every charge to be brought to the table. Since I was just a juvenile, they could only give me seven years until my twenty-first birthday. That was the sentence that the judge handed down. "T.Y.C."(Texas Youth Council)

Gatesville, Texas Reformatory, is a penal institution for young offenders. Boy, it was nothing nice, not at Mountain View. It was maximum at the juvenile facility. Everybody was in for the same thing I was, so it got pretty hard in there. At first, it seemed like forever. Then, all of a sudden, a month before my eighteenth birthday, I was given five years parole. That morning at 10:30 a.m., I said a prayer, "God, help me to do good." I wanted to start a new life, so I left it at that.

It wasn't long before I got in trouble again. I saw one of the boys that had been locked up with me when I was walking. He picked me up and asked me if I wanted a ride. I said, "Sure, why not?" A few blocks down the road, the cops showed up with lights on. I said, "Just be cool," but he said, "The car is hot." Oh man! I didn't need this. Of course, I went back to jail. I asked God, "Can You get me out of this, please?" I didn't have to go to court. Somehow, God had made them lose my paperwork.

I forgot all about the time I did when I hooked up with my boys. Before you know it, I was back in the game, pulling robberies and shooting dope. I got caught up in some murders.

There I was, facing forty-five to life. I was in jail, and I started a gang in the jailhouse. It was automatic. Man, after two years in there waiting for my cases to come to court, I was getting tired of this life. You know, it gets old. I was looking for something like a change of life. I just didn't know how.

Then one day, I found myself at the library, when Sister Margaret asked me, "Can I help you?" I said, "Yeah. I don't want to hear about God, or anything like that."She asked, "Something to read? Like what?" "Well, something like gangsters. Here I am trying to get out of the gang thing and got right back into it," I replied. Man! But God is always on time, you know — never late and always right on time.

Anyway, she said, "I have just the book for you." "Really?" I said. She explained, "Yes, I'm pretty sure you will like it." It was about some guy named Nicky Cruz. *The Cross and the Switchblade* is a story about a gangster from New York

City. I got to reading this book, stopped about three times and started reading it all over again. In this book, it looked like I was reading about me! So I stopped for a minute, and said, "God, I wish You could change me like You changed Nicky." I finished reading the book. In the back of it was a prayer inviting Jesus into your heart as Lord and Savior, so I did. After that, I didn't think about my cases. I left it all to God.

Time went by fast. It was time for sentencing, and I was waiting for the judge to hand it down. All of a sudden, the D.A. stood up and said, "Your Honor, if it pleases the court, may I have a word with the defendants?" The judge said, "Well, I never heard of such a thing, but since you represent the state of Texas, I don't see why not. I'll give you twenty minutes."

We went into this room, and the D.A. offers to change the charges so that the sentences would go from forty-five years, down to seven years. He said, "If you cop to all these charges, I will close the book, and give you three seven-year terms running together." There were four of us, and one of my full partners said, "If we fight, we could win." I looked at him for a minute and said, "I don't know, man. A chance like this doesn't come very often." Because we were all guilty, and we knew it, we took the three seven- year terms running together.

God did a big miracle for us. I thank Him and praise His Holy name for everything He did. The way I see it, our Father used the D.A. as our defense attorney. So, to T.D.C. it was.

During the fourth year of my sentence, the Lord was working another miracle for me in one of the worst penitentiaries in the United States. You see, there were a lot of killings during the time I was there. The Fed's planted some of their people in the Eastham Unit of T.D.C., to find out why there were so many killings, and so many people disappearing.

One day, we were working out in the field, and this dude walked up to me and said, "Hey, Jess, there's a hit out tonight." And my answer was, "There's always a hit out.""Yeah," he said. "But this one has your name on it." No one wants to die, especially on the inside. I started praying and asking Jesus to let me make it to my cell, so I could be alone with Him. I just kept praying coming in from the fields: through the showers, through chow hall, and down the hall, to P Line, where I had lived for seven years.

I made it, got down on my knees and said, "You know, Lord, these people never miss their man. They always get them. So, I come to you, Lord Jesus. I know I have not lived exactly the way you wanted me to. I didn't think I was going to die here. I ask you to please forgive me of all my sins, so if I die tonight, I can be with you. If they cripple me, I just want to make it right with you, Lord. People say you speak to us through the Scriptures. I have a New Testament book here, so I need for you to speak to me right now. I need to hear from you, so when I open this book, please speak to me."

I picked up the New Testament, and when I opened it, my eyes looked right at *Matthew 6:25-26 "Do not worry,"* stared right at me, and I received it; just what it said in the Scripture. Thank you, Lord! All of a sudden, a peace came over me, and it was like someone had told me it was going to be just fine.

Everybody was asking me if I was coming out, and I said, "Yeah, I am coming out." All this time, there was a man standing to the right of my cell. I couldn't see him. No one was saying anything. You see, with gangs, there's no honor. Really you can be a loyal soldier to them, but there is always hatred, jealousy, dissension, envy, and fits of rage. Between the cracks, it looks good from the outside, but there is always someone waiting to take you out, just like in the Italian mafia. They kill their own just for territorial power.

This man was waiting for them to call in and out, meaning come out for mail call. They called - the third row, then the second row came out. I lived on the first row and was waiting to come out when this man jumped out in front of me. There he stood, staring at me with a shank in his hand. It was about ten inches long. He could have gotten me, but my cell door didn't open. All the rest of the doors opened except mine. While this was happening, it was like he couldn't move. God just stopped him in his tracks, because he didn't move at all. Anyway, the guards came, got him, and took him to the hole.

Meanwhile, the guard called the maintenance man to see what was wrong with the cell door because they couldn't get it opened. The maintenance man said, "There isn't anything wrong with the door. It should be working." So they just left it alone, and all of a sudden my door opened. I walked out as if nothing had happened. The trustee asked me how I got out. I replied, "My door opened." "No way," he said. Then, he looked up to the third row where the guard was. The guard asked, "How did you get out?" I told them the door opened. There was no other way for that to have happened except for the Lord God of Abraham, the God of Isaac, and the God of Jacob. Amen. And from that day on, when the men there at Eastham Unit saw me, they talked among themselves like they were afraid of me. I had a lot of respect. All the glory goes to my God Jesus Christ. Stay true to Him. Obey Him in everything because He's the only one that keeps His promises. The Lord said, *"I will never leave you nor forsake you." (Joshua 1:5b)*

14. A CHRISTMAS STORY IN JAIL — Carlos Tanguma

A few months ago, while I was in the "hole," I asked God, "Lord, when are you going to let me go from this jail?" "I have a few more things to teach you first," was His response. These "lessons" are always about people, you and me.

In the weeks leading up to Christmas, my funds and supplies ran out, and long-promised money just hadn't come. Yes, I've gone broke and have been without supplies many times in the fifteen months I've served here at ACDF. Though, the holidays accentuated my dilemma. I've found through searching God's Word and through faith, prayer, and patience that He provides more than what I need. My money order still hadn't come as Christmas dawned, and I started bumming coffee. God allowed me to become so broke again after providing so much.

I've never seen so many indigent people in any of the six

pods, but the "Maximum Saints" in F1300 just weren't willing to ignore their Christmas spirit which is the gift of Jesus Christ from God to everyone. They reminded me through their selfless actions that we are all capable of doing good. These guys made sure every one of us got a gift from the commissary list. I got a donut. It was an awesome donut because in this instance, it symbolized to me God's love, grace, and mercy which is in our hearts, primed and beating for us to show the world!

There was a healing glow on the faces of these selfless givers and Christmas cheer as they passed out presents to the less fortunate. It was time for the Secret Santa gift unwrapping for which they had drawn names. One man, who sports a clean shaven head, unwrapped a comb and a shower cap! No, Christmas was not forgotten in F1300 this year. Had we had a Christmas tree or a mantel from which to hang holiday stockings, their cheer would have been overshadowed by the smiles, laughter and brotherly love we experienced that morning.

Jesus said, *"For I was hungry and you gave me something to eat, I was thirsty and you gave me something to drink, I was a stranger and you invited me in, I needed clothes and you clothed me, I was sick and you looked after me, I was in prison and you came to visit me....The King will reply, 'I tell you the truth, whatever you did for one of the least of these brothers of mine, you did for me."* (Matthew 25:35-40) Jesus is in you and in me. Let Him show you that everything is in His hands and that His hands are everywhere. This act of selfless giving was a miracle, friend. Miracles are a glimpse of what paradise is like: no sorrow, no pain, and no suffering. I received my money order about an hour after my Christmas donut, and in comparison, the donut shines brighter than gold.

15. PLOWING THE HARD GROUND OF THE HEART
— Marvin Hatcher

In the course of the thirty-five years of my Christianity, I have lived almost entirely behind a Christian mask. I did indeed have a true conversion to Christ when I was younger, but several years afterward, I developed a pocket of sin in my life that I had never truly repented. As a result, I fell headlong into what *James 1:14-15* warns us about. *"But each one is tempted when, by his own evil desire, he is dragged away and enticed. Then, after desire has conceived, it gives birth to sin; and sin, when it is full-grown, gives birth to death."* Two years ago, my sin grew up and gave birth to death in my life. Not only was I dead spiritually all those years back, but two years ago, my sin killed everything in my life that I had held precious and dear to me.

My fourteen year marriage was over because of a restraining order from my wife. I have been prohibited to see her as well as my children. I lost my beautiful, newly-built house and everything that I had accumulated in the last fourteen years. Six months ago, I lost my job, and now I have lost my freedom. Sin grew up in my life and stripped me of everything, including my identity of who I used to be in Christ. Devastation, heartache, depression, and loneliness were all that I could call my own.

God finally had me where he wanted me, stripped of everything except the knowledge that my God was still the Savior of my soul, ever merciful, ever loving, and ever with me if I would only just ask Him back into my life. Six months ago, when I came to ACDF, I did just that. I poured myself into the hands of my living God. I saturated my mind with the Word of God. I began talking to God like I had never talked to Him ever before in my life.

He brought fellow inmates across my path for me to speak into their lives the great and wonderful things that God is doing in mine. I began to see God do amazing things in the inmates around me. Every day was a brand new experience of what God was doing in our pod. It was at this point that I began hearing God's voice speaking specifically to me, deep in my innermost being.

One night, I awoke in the middle of the night to God's voice encouraging me. He told me how much He loved me, that

I was truly His son, and to be encouraged. God told me that I would soon be released, that I would serve Him all the days of my life here on earth, and that He has a wonderful future planned for me. I was thrilled to hear His voice, so I started to ask Him if I could also be transferred to F pod. Before I could finish my request to Him, I heard Him chuckle and say, "Yes, you may go to F Module." Eventually, because of our overcrowding, I was sent to F Module. My faith just soared into the sky. Right then and there, I knew that if this one thing came to pass, then His promise of my release was soon on its way.

I began to understand that being sent to this jail cell was not so much punishment as it was a powerful new beginning. Where I was at, at that very moment in time, here in this jail, was the most wonderful experience of my entire life. I knew that I had reached the bottom in my life, and God had met me right at the most broken place in my life. Given over to Him totally, I was on an exciting new road. I was immersing myself in prayer and in the Word of God more than I ever had before.

Several nights before my final court date for sentencing, I was praying, when all of a sudden He spoke these words to me, "I think that you will be the last one down there." I was the last one to be called at the court, and I envisioned God's presence in the center of the courtroom, influencing everyone there. God was in charge, and I believed that I soon would be put back out on probation again. I was simply overjoyed that God's promise to release me was finally here. I was called into the courtroom and stood in front of the judge with my public defender at my side. The judge allowed me a few words before sentencing me.

To my surprise, the judge got very stern with me, scolded me for the crime that I had committed, and proceeded to sentence me to four years at D.O.C.. All the blood ran out of my face, and an icy cold shock ran through my body. I was stunned. On the bus trip back to the jail, I was still in shock, but I had an uncanny peace that blanketed me. Instinctively I knew it was the peace of Jesus that passes all understanding.

God spoke to me once more right at that time, "Did you really think it would be that easy? You are still on the journey Will you still trust me?" Of course, I immediately said, "Yes, Lord, I will trust you for my journey with you." I learned a very important lesson that day. Certainly, God was encouraging me in the course of imprisonment in this jail cell, and He was raising my hopes of His planned future for my life. But as with the permission that He gave me to be transferred to F Module, I did not get there according to my time table nor according to how I thought I would get there. I did not learn God's lesson then, and I did not learn God's lesson for my sentencing that day. God truly spoke to me all right, but I made the mistake of taking His words and running ahead, calculating my own version of when and how God was going to fulfill those promises. Sadly, God had to yank me back down to earth and remind me that He wanted to be God in my life, not me.

A couple of days later, Chaplain came to talk to me. After the bus trip back to jail two days before, there was a huge painful gap in my heart with the great question of, "Why?" Until I met her, I was vexed with that question. She said many encouraging things to me that day, and the better part of an hour went by. At the end of that hour she said something so profound to me that I knew God was speaking to me through her.

God answered that gnawing question, "Why?" The answer came in two parts. The first part was that I was second guessing God in His promises to me. In reality, I have absolutely no idea how God is maneuvering things in my life. Chaplain told me that so many times we make the mistake of preconceiving God's hand in our lives. When God gives us a word, we jump ahead of His prescribed path that He has us on and create our own idea of how God will answer our needs. She said that instead, we need to wait for God to grant us what He wills in our lives, not to look past God, but instead to patiently look only to God. In due time, He will cause us to arrive when and where He wants us to be, eliminating any heartache, disappointment, and frustrations that are created. The second part of what Chaplain shared with me was nothing short of pure revelation from God.

God spoke to me that my heart is like an unplowed field. Hard-packed earth cannot receive seeds for planting, and nothing can grow in it. He told me that I had areas of my heart that still remained unplowed, that until my heart would undergo more plowing so that He could plant more seeds of His righteousness in me, I would remain on this journey to my freedom. It would only be then that I could enjoy the fulfilling of His promise of freedom in my life. I thanked the chaplain for being obedient in speaking God's word to my life, and told her that the huge gap of "Why?" was now filled and answered completely. I now understand that the judge's decision was really God's choice for me. God is preparing the future of my life right here at this jail, and soon to be at D.O.C., by plowing up my heart so that I can grow in His maturity and power for my life. I can now see a real purpose for the judge's decision. All I can say now is that God must have some astounding future planned for me!

16. GOD SPOKE TO ME — Teresa Rhodes

I had seen God speak to people around me, and I begged Him to speak to me directly. I asked my husband how he first knew that God spoke to him. He told me he has always known since he was very little. He said, "He speaks to all of us. Maybe you're just not listening." After that I tried hard to listen. I was mad because my husband could hear Him, and I couldn't. I begged God to send me something very loud – like a burning bush or something I couldn't mistake.

Shortly after this, I got put in jail. I was in a worship and the minister, Carol, said she had something prepared but God had just spoken to her and was changing her sermon. She spoke that day about the truth that will set you free. Whoa! I was sure that message wasn't for me because I was on my seventh revocation on probation, and I had committed yet another crime. I had stolen a "Pokeman" watch for my roommate, but I wasn't caught red-handed! I had my lie ready. Not only would the truth not set me free, I'd be in the pen for sure if I told the truth!

The next few days, I was bombarded with things saying – the truth will set you free: the TV, KLOVE radio station, and people talking. I didn't want to hear it, because I was sure it wasn't true! I thought the devil was tricking me into going to prison. The morning of court, however, I had finally realized it was God speaking to me. I decided God must want me to go to prison, and I told God, because I loved Him, I would go. I would tell the truth in court.

That morning my probation officer talked forever about how horrible I was and that prison was the only answer. The D.A. stood silent. The judge asked me to tell my side. I told the truth and waited for my sentence. I felt a beautiful peace over me! The judge not only set me free that moment, but also cancelled my last three years of probation. He said he didn't see what prison could do for me. He said he was going to set me totally free and then, if I got into trouble after all, he would see me again and remember this day. He said he hoped I had learned my lesson and that I would be good. I have been good, and I have listened for God to speak. Over the last four years, I have seen that His plans are always better than mine! I've learned to seek God's wisdom in all situations, and it's been a non-stop adventure!

17. THE LORD POURED HIS LOVE INTO ME
— Gregory Ulrich

I tried to quit drinking because I knew it would cause me more problems, but I couldn't do it. I drank myself into a coma. A month later, seeing a few different women, I got my third D.U.I. I wish I could tell you I learned my lesson, but nope, not yet. One month later in a drunken fit, I drove into a light pole, and just then two young bodies lost their souls. Not realizing what I had done, I was lying in the hospital with a broken femur bone, five broken ribs, and a collapsed lung when my girlfriend JP came to my side.

Ten days later, two detectives arrested me for a warrant in Adams County for probation violations. I was depressed and miserable, so I was assigned to the medical unit. Two days went by, and I was called back to booking. That was when they advised me of my charges in Jefferson County: vehicular homicide, two counts; vehicular homicide reckless driving, two counts; D.U.I., two counts; driving under restraint; and driving without insurance.

My heart went to my throat and tears came to my eyes. I was allowed a free phone call. I called the only person I could think of at that moment, JP. She wasn't home, but I left a sobbing message on her machine. I told her I was sorry and to forget about me, that I was probably going to spend the next twenty to thirty years in prison. On my way back to medical, I prayed to the Lord to place me in a cell with men of God! I was then placed with two older fellows, Mac and Frosty. I was miserable and depressed. I was confined to a wheelchair, and I couldn't eat or sleep. I couldn't even put my clothes on by myself. Thanks to God, these two fellows helped me a lot. They were men of God! (Thanks, guys!)

Feeling so bad for what I had done, and how miserable my life was before the accident, I contemplated killing myself and how to do it. I felt I had no reason to live. One of the men gave me a Bible. I started reading and talking to God all through the days. Within a week of being in jail, to my surprise, JP sent me a letter full of Scriptures, telling me how she cared for me and to trust in God! That stopped me from killing myself. She made me think that God kept me alive for a reason. When I saw pictures of my accident, where two of my passengers had died even though they wore their seatbelts, I realized there was no way I should have survived.

Weeks later, I got classified to F2200. And again on the way up, I prayed to be put in with good, godly people, and I was put in directly with the godly people of F2200. We started a prayer group. God really started pouring His love into me. I had never felt anything as powerful as what I was feeling. I was still very much depressed for being responsible for killing two people, and I was having a hard time forgiving myself for what I had done. The group saw that and helped me come to the fact that Jesus died for my sins. I asked God to come into my heart and free me of my sins and pain. One day, I heard that I had no right not to forgive myself. At that moment, I felt the Lord pour His love into me. I wept. I truly felt as though I was born again!

18. YOU MUST DO THE WORK OF GOD
— Brandon Pettigrew

What I will tell you about is one instance of hatred in my life and how God reached out and touched me. On my sentencing date, I was expecting to go to prison. The courts told me I was not eligible for probation or for community corrections because of the violent nature of my case. God was with me in that courtroom. The victim of my crimes came to my sentencing date. He told the judge that he forgave me for what I had done to him and that he wanted me to have another chance. The damage I did to that man was serious. It changed the way he had to live his life. But still, he forgave me. That is God's work. Only God is capable of changing people's hearts like that. God gave me another chance. I got probation for four years.

Now, I am back. I have new, more serious charges. God gave me another chance, and I took it for granted. How foolish of me. I realize now that just believing and praying is not enough. You must do the work of the Lord. You must actively be involved in ministry. You must tell people about the good of God. You must help others selflessly. We are in a spiritual battle. If we stop fighting for one minute, Satan will take the opportunity to seize us. If you do not strive everyday to live as Jesus did and to obey God's Word, then you will fail and fall into your own ways, the ways of the world. If you choose to serve God, it is a choice for the rest of eternity. You cannot go back. You cannot remain idle. If you do, you will end up back here, like me. If you choose God, you have to be ready to uphold your end of the deal, because He always upholds His end. If you don't, there is a price to pay. *"It is better not to vow than to make a vow and not fulfill it."* (Ecclesiastes 5:5)

19. YES, JESUS LOVES ME — Jason Vigil

A life that could only be described as a nightmare — that was my life. From adolescence to early adulthood I lived in sin, knowing full well I was wrong, but nonetheless, I persevered on the path of unrighteousness. All I wanted to do was drink, get high, and participate in gang activity. I had little regard for others (that I consequently hurt) and none at all for myself. I was a menace to society. I was in and out of detention facilities my entire adolescence. I was a druggie at an early age, smoking marijuana and using coke on a daily basis. I was abusing my body, God's temple. I can't say that I was ignorant because I was acting on my own volition.

I was sent to prison at the age of eighteen for stealing cars, and still I was blind to the fact that I was never alone – though that's how I felt, completely alone. I didn't know that true peace and happiness could only be found through Jesus. I sought comfort in being part of a gang because I so foolishly felt that they were the only ones that cared. But, as I was in and out of jails and prisons, I found that the gang could care less about my salvation. I emotionally secluded myself from family and so—called friends, except for my loving girlfriend Marla. It was just Marla and me!

I still felt empty inside and began using heroine intravenously to try to block out all the horrible feelings of loneliness, but all it did was make problems worse. I became sick with cotton fever from the drugs and almost died on three separate occasions, once in my little brother's arms. Fortunately, I survived, and only because the Lord said, "No, Jason, it's not your time yet." I was locked up shortly after my twenty-third birthday, and, withdrawing from heroine, I went through the most horrid pain one could endure. But thank God, I made it!

When I got out of jail, I found that Marla was still very much plagued by that horrible heroine demon. I did all I could to convince her to get off the drugs, but to no avail. We had an argument; I left her and went off and did my own thing (gang banging). About a month after our argument, Marla got locked up for thirty days and withdrew from the heroine. I was ecstatic! We became good friends again and talked regularly, and I found myself coming up with reasons to go to her aunt's house, just so I could make sure she didn't relapse and was really okay.

The night I last saw her, we got into another argument, and I left yet again and joined up with so-called friends. That very night I was arrested for participating in gang activity and ended up in Adams County Jail facing ten to thirty-two years in the penitentiary. I was beyond distraught, and thought to myself, "Things can't possibly get any worse." And then, four days after my incarceration, my Marla died from an overdose of heroine.

Certain individuals in my cellblock tried to assure me that Marla was in a better place and was better off than any of us; but I wasn't hearing it. I was mad at God, and now I regret some of what I said to the Lord about what happened to Marla. A month and a half after her passing, I got out of "segregation" and was moved to a different maximum-security cellblock, celled-up with a man by the name of Michah Collins. I shared with him all the horrendous events of my life, especially the recent ones. He began ministering to me little by little, and soon I came out of my emotional state of solitude. I began loving and praising God! At that time, I began to see clearly, and believed in my heart that Marla Rose was indeed in a better place, the Heavenly Kingdom!

Shortly after this, my brother in Christ, Michah Collins, gave me a book called *A Divine Revelation of Hell*, by Mary Baxter. In this book, I read about a great many souls enduring the punishment of eternal damnation for not coming to the Lord and confessing that Jesus is Lord, and receiving Him as their Lord and Savior, while they were alive. About halfway through this book, I became scared that Marla might be suffering eternally in hell, for not coming to the Lord for her salvation, simply because the whole time we were together, she never prayed, much less even mentioned the Lord Jesus.

I went on for days worrying about Marla and her salvation, praying to God that she wasn't in hell. "She doesn't deserve hell," I would plead. Then one day, Michah came to me with another book called *Maximum Saints Never Hide in the Dark*. He showed me an article called "A Friend Named Marla," written by a woman that had met Marla the time she went to jail. Michah heard a voice saying, "Bring it to Jason." At first, he didn't know that it was about my Marla, although indeed it was! After I read the article, I brought it back to him with tears in my eyes, tears of joy because it told about how Marla had met another Christian in jail and had gotten saved prior to her passing.

It was reassurance to me that Marla is with the Lord in the Kingdom of Heaven. God answered my prayer and showed me through Michah that Marla is in His safekeeping—a miracle in my eyes! So rejoice, my brothers and sisters in Christ, the Lord does answer the prayers of those who love Him. *"And we know that in all things God works for the good of those who love him, who have been called according to His purpose."* (Romans 8:28)

20. I CAN'T POSSIBLY TURN FROM MY CHRIST JESUS
— Jesse Castro

I just received five years in the Department of Corrections for a car theft. The purpose of this testimony is to acknowledge that before I received these five years in D.O.C., I continually prayed to God, asking Him, at times begging Him and crying to Him, to forgive me for my sins and to help me overcome the facts of why I was incarcerated to begin with.

I'm a substance abuser who has struggled with thoughts of losing family members and thoughts of being out on the streets. Here I am: locked up not only within a concrete cell, but bound within deep, dark secrets of sin (which come back to haunt me) as the long hours of lockdown drag on. I was facing sixteen to twenty-four years. Anyway, a big war story of what I did out on the streets is not important. What I went through by praying to Christ Jesus to ease my suffering is what I want to write about.

Isn't it odd how we seem to worship, praise or acknowledge our Father God only when we're in trouble? Can anyone tell me why it is I have chosen to do such? When I cannot or do not have control over a situation, I turn to Father God. It's times like these that I want to pray to Christ Jesus. When I sit within a concrete cell is the only time that I agree I have problems. Have I lived inappropriately? Doing drugs isn't that bad! There are worse people than I, but they are not me. How common it is to point the finger and judge others, not seeing that I'm the one. "Hello, McFly," who is in jail? No! I can't face this! My immoral thoughts! My tainted life of pride! The false beliefs of darkness blinded me into thinking everything was okay.

I actually believed that I could do the crime and do the time. But not this time! How embarrassing it is to be considered a man and to not even be able to live life on life's terms. I need to be placed in a cell like a wild pit bull needs to remain chained. Being the person that I am, I can easily pretend to have some pride and not ridicule myself because it is not really that bad.

If I didn't see what this really is, I wouldn't be real with myself. I'd act as if all was okay because I'm strong—I'm a convict. True convicts don't do hard time. True convicts don't bow down. True convicts fail to see that the pattern will never change until they break off a healthy chunk of their lives, if not the rest of their lives.

Again, isn't it odd how those situations occur in order to bring us closer to God? I seriously thought I had broken off at least fifteen years of my life this time. I should've received more than what I did. I remember before I went to court, I prayed to

Lord Jesus to help me, Lord Jesus save me, Lord Jesus this, and Lord Jesus that. I mean I prayed for me, I prayed for you, the moon, the stars, the sun, my family, your family, the dog, the cat and whatever else a person who's desperate can think of praying for.

I was in the holding tank with two other men who believed in God but weren't of Christian beliefs. We all had motion hearings, and we were all in the same boat when it came to the wheeling and dealing of how many years would be spent in prison. I believed that my Jesus was with me. I pulled out my prayer book and completely blocked them out. They wanted to pray, too, all of a sudden.

I don't know what happened in their cases, but I do know that when we were in that tank, all fear of what we didn't know came to pass. Our prayer cleansed the air and at the last minute, I gained confidence that Father God would make His will known through the words I spoke to the judge.

He gave me the strength to properly vocalize empathy, righteousness, wisdom and sincerity. I suffered a great deal of humility while up at the podium because I admitted to the judge all my wrongs, my struggles, and my crooked beliefs which had led me to jail time after time. I mentioned that I turned my life over to God. I was aware of a sinful nature that existed within me, and how the Apostle Paul has influenced my life to remain in union with Christ Jesus. I can't explain to you how relieved I felt when he said only five years. Five years! Five years ain't nothing. I could do that standing on my head. I'll be out in less than a year. To think all this time, I was trippin' over nothing. They didn't have anything to begin with anyway.

Hold up! Can you see the sudden change in my attitude, my sudden boost of pride, my ungratefulness to Lord Jesus Christ? I'm sure if I didn't want my Jesus, I could easily turn away, but He has shown me that He is real through visions of faith! Obedience to Christ Jesus has indeed made me realize He will not allow me to experience more than what I can bear. Just think for a minute, what if I weren't grateful for this beautiful outcome of only five years?

Never mind. I don't even want to think of how much I would be tortured by the demons in hell. To think that I almost made the decision to turn away from my Christ Jesus after I had used Him to get what I needed. To think that I became tainted with pride again: the arrogant convict mentality easily welcomed me back with open arms. I had almost forgotten all those sleepless nights on my knees with the lump in my throat and the silent cries which were the tears falling down my face.

Do I feel ashamed for writing that I literally cried like a helpless man, hoping I would walk away from this? No. Through my prayers, through my studies, through my belief, my Christ Jesus has saved me. Through obedience, I shall continue to be a child of God.

The Holy Spirit fills my heart in ways I can't possibly explain to you, my brothers. I can't possibly turn from my Christ Jesus. I have so much more to learn, and I need to remain a faithful apprentice to the Holy Trinity. I remain desperate for the teachings of the Bible, for I thirst for my Jesus. Through the grace of the Holy Trinity, may I continue to transform into a disciple of God. *"He who has an ear let him hear what the Spirit says to the churches."(Revelation 2:11a) "Trust in the Lord with all your heart and lean not on your own understanding; in all your ways acknowledge him, and he will make your paths straight."(Proverbs 3:5 -6)* God bless you.

21. DON'T TURN YOUR BACK ON HIM — Jose Garcia

One Sunday, I told the chaplain I was going to give my testimony at Chaplain's Worship in two weeks. But in those two weeks I lost my wife to the world of her deception and cheating with another man. So, coming here to worship, I was grieving for the loss of someone who was very dear to me. I was having second thoughts about giving my testimony. I searched within myself, and I asked my God to give me the strength to go up there and tell you my story.

I've been coming in and out of jail, and progressing in giving my life to my Lord Jesus Christ. Whenever I was released, I would go back to the devil's work. My drug, rock cocaine, was destroying my life. I was dragging my wife down with me as I manipulated her to get more drugs.

The last time I was incarcerated in the beginning of November 2001, for domestic violence, again I surrendered my life to my God: receiving the Holy Spirit and also receiving the gift of healing with prayer. My brother had been diagnosed with colon cancer, and I prayed for him to be healed. The next day he was in remission. Thanks be to God!

But I didn't really understand about the Holy Spirit. I was arrested again on the charge of domestic violence, let out on bail, and still chose to get lost in the world of destruction. I was still smoking rock cocaine, not knowing when to quit. I was causing arguments with my wife, having money problems, but I was not motivated to work it out. I didn't listen to my wife when she was crying out to me to stop what I was doing. I landed up in jail again, picked up by undercover cops for failure to appear. Coming to jail, in F1100, I saw my brother in-law. I knew him out in the free world: I saw him so differently this time, as though there was a bright light over him. Then he told me, "I was waiting for you." I asked, "How did you know I was coming?" He said, "The Lord told me!" He had given his life to God.

The next morning I was looking for him, and he was going to different cubicles, getting different Scriptures from different people. I sat down to listen, still thinking of getting out and doing my drug. Then he asked me, "Do you want a Bible? I have an extra." I replied, "No, I am getting out in two or three months." Then he said, "Don't put off until tomorrow what you could do today!" So then I took the Bible and got back into the Word. I was anxious to get where I had been the last time. I had given my life to the Lord, and had been going to church. Attending Chaplain's Worship Services every Saturday, I was learning about the Pentecost, the Holy Spirit, and the spiritual condition. By choosing to meditate on Scriptures, applying them to our lives and following God's standard for our thinking, we will live in a way that pleases the Father. We will become the people He planned for us to be, and accomplish His purposes for us.

My communication with my God grew stronger. In the Bible it says to be honest and truthful with yourself and others, and the truth will set you free. I was in denial about my drug habit. But when I read that, I started to open up about my drug problem, and I started to work on it. I started to go to classes like Drug Ed., N.A., and so forth. God knows everything and sees everything. I was hiding my addiction from the courts, but not any more. I want to be set free: not only from jail, but also from my own destruction.

I started to work on my character. One area I knew I had to work on was my impatience. I needed to be healed of an old wound received from a past relationship. I was using the drugs to numb my pain caused by my wife in the past. This got me even closer to my God. I gave Him all my pain, worries, stress — my everything. Turning it all over to God, I gave Him my whole life.

Then one night in a vision, I saw a demon in one of my peers, and the devil was telling me, "I want you. You are mine." I was scared, and I called out, " In the name of Jesus, in the name of Jesus, rebuke the evil spirit away. He is not wanted here." Covering my head with my blanket in fear, I felt tears coming down my face. My God called on me, and He said, "Do not fear, I am here, my son." I had already received the Holy Spirit, but I didn't understand it. In that moment I did. I felt such peace, joy, contentment, and was very happy. I asked my God to forgive me for all my sins and to cleanse me. He then told me that I had the gift of healing with prayer: I have immense compassion for others, but that the Holy Spirit would teach me how to use the gift in the right way.

When I came to jail this time, I was changing my life so my wife wouldn't leave me, but now I am changing for me. I was beating myself down before because I thought it was all my fault, but now I see things more clearly. Yes, I have some faults. But I have to learn from my mistakes, and own them, so I won't stumble over the same faults again. I give thanks to my God for staying by me all the way. God is always there if you call on him. He never deserts you. He loves you. Don't turn your back on Him. When I get released and walk out of this place, I am going to walk out with my head up with my Lord Jesus Christ right next to me.

22. I HAVE FOUND MY CALLING — Daniel Skaife

I'd like to tell you about how I was "found." I was born into a very loving family. However, as I grew from childhood into adolescence, my life turned out very "differently" than I expected. I got into dangerous drugs, theft, and running away - running away physically as well as mentally. I don't know what I was running from!

My loving father, whom I've always admired, was a minister for a church in Casper, Wyoming. That's where I first gave myself to the Lord. In spite of this, before long I found myself in trouble. In 1987, I was convicted of burglary and sent to the penitentiary for eight years. It was a waste of time, for nothing changed.

In 1994, I was discharged from the penitentiary. I stayed clean for twelve years. However, I was still oblivious to following the path of righteousness. I was still blessed, for I met a very special woman during this time; my soul mate. She came into my life and showed me what true love looks like. Things were looking up. Then, I ran into an old friend! Again, I got into trouble, and that's what put me where I am today (in jail.)

When I arrived at the Adams County Jail in 2006, I was classified as a "maximum" security inmate. At first, when I entered the "max" pod, I was moved into a cell with a man that had nothing but bitterness in his heart. Upon my arrival, I met two people that helped me to see clearly. Three days later, though, I was introduced to Michah Collins and Jason Vigil, who later became my cellmate (thank the Lord!).

As days turned to weeks, I noticed that Michah and Jason were doing the Lord's bidding by sharing the Gospel, and right then I wanted to get my life on the right track - the path of righteousness. I received a Bible and dove right in! I repented of my sins and asked the Lord's forgiveness. Consequently, I believe in my heart, I have received forgiveness, praise the Lord! I began doing Bible studies of my own as well as praying to the Lord in all my endeavors, casting all my worries upon Him. *(1 Peter 5:7)*

Then one day, Michah walked up to me and said, "God's gonna bless you." At the time I had no idea the impact that would have on me—for God did bless me. The court gave me halfway house time as opposed to prison time. I was blessed with a new start. I can feel the Holy Spirit, and the magic of regeneration, working within my heart!

Jason and I talk a lot about the Bible and how loving Jesus helps when things may not be going your way. I learned from the Holy Scripture to bring all my concerns to the Lord, for it says, *"Ask and it will be given to you."(Matthew 7:7)* REJOICE, my brothers in Christ, for when one puts his faith and trust in God, things always work out for the good: *"And we know that in all things God works for the good of those who love him." (Romans 8:28a)* I thank those two men that brought the love of God into my heart: Michah and Jason. May God shine down upon you both. Amen.

23. LOOK AT CHRIST, YOU WILL BE AT REST
— Margaret Jones

I'll never forget that night, the look of disappointment my father had on his face thinking I was messing up again and broke my promises. It was a holiday weekend, so I had to wait until Tuesday to go to advisors. A friend and my dad were there. Then I had to go back a week later for a bond reduction which I was denied because I didn't have a lawyer by my side. The same friend and my father were there again.

Who would have known that that was going to be the last time I'd see my father alive? He died the very next day of a massive heart attack. He was going to be cooking us spaghetti the next night after that for us, as a welcome home between him and I, cause spaghetti is my favorite besides his chili.

The day my dad died, I ran back into the pod crying and one of the other girls tried to comfort me, telling me not to worry that he was now in a much better place with God! "Yea, right," is what I thought. I screamed out, "There is no God! He doesn't exist." My goodness, if looks could have killed without catching another case, I'd be one dead white girl! I totally felt all eyes on me and at that moment I knew I made a mistake by saying that aloud. It only took a few days for one of the other ladies to come to me with standing in our pod's prayer circle. Then, before I knew it, she talked and persuaded me into a Bible study with her and some other ladies.

Thank you, Yolanda, for helping me. You are a God sent angel! When I think of her, I think of *James 5:19-20*, *"My brothers, if one of you should wander from the truth and someone should bring him back, remember this: Whoever turns a sinner from the error of his way will save him from death and cover over a multitude of sins."* Boy, let me tell you. That's exactly what she did to me. We started a Bible study, that was a 40 day study called, *The Purpose Driven Life*, by Rick Warren. I'm currently on day 31, and during those past days, here is what I've learned: Don't give up, grow up! *Romans 8:28-29, "And we know that in all things God works for the good of those who love Him, who have been called according to His purpose. For those God foreknew, He also predestined to be conformed to the likeness of his Son, that he might be the first born among many brothers."*

Being incarcerated, I couldn't take care of my father's body, so I had him in the ice box for 6 weeks. Eventually I had to let him go. "Thank you, Daddy, for caring and loving me so much. I'm sorry for all of our fights, and for not being there when you opened your eyes while waiting for surgery. I'm also sorry you had to stay in the ice box so long. I know how much you hated being so cold, putting the heat up to 90 degrees in the middle of summer when we were back home in New York and Jersey! But today is the day, 6 weeks later, you are finally being cremated and laid to rest."

I cannot imagine what Corrie Ten Boom was going through in a Nazi concentration camp and I thought for sure the trouble I was facing was nothing compared. Well, being that I'm so new to all this, I feel as if I am the baby of the group. My sisters in Christ: Melissa, Ashley, Rita, Dianna, Yolanda, Ms. Charleboix, Renee, Evangelina and, believe it or not, even Edy. These women have helped me through so much: to stay focused, to stay strong, and have encouraged me to stay with God's Word! I came across this saying when studying. It is called, "The power of focus." If you look at the world, you'll be distressed. If you look within, you'll be depressed. But if you look at Christ, you'll be at rest.

24. THE BIBLE AND ME — Steve Griffin

The Bible has affected me in many different ways in my short walk with Jesus. I found the Lord about seven months ago. I have never felt so calm, and have new peace within. I feel like there's nothing I cannot do as I walk with the Lord — nothing seems impossible anymore.

Ever since I have been a believer, all of my needs have been met: food, shelter, physical and mental support. My faith in God has brought my family a lot closer to me than ever before. I know they can see that my heart has turned around for good. They can truly see the change even though they have not seen me in person. They can tell by my voice over the phone that I am not the same person anymore. And, that right there has been a blessing. I used to only think about myself before I found God.

I used to have a lot of cravings for alcohol. Now, I study on a regular basis and there are none of those cravings at all anymore. Even though I am still just beginning to learn about God and all He can do, I feel nothing but love and support. I do not worry as I put all faith in the Heavenly Father. By this faith, I have all that I need because no matter what happens, He will not lead me astray. That's how I know everything will be all right in Jesus' name.

25. THEY OPENED MY EYES TO SEE — Daniel Lopez

I am twenty-four years old, from Dallas, Texas, and just moved to Colorado about three years ago. I have been in and out of different jails in different states. I grew up around drugs and alcohol. Basically, I knew what drugs were before I could count. My father, and my uncles, were all into drug trafficking. So, now you know why I came to live in Colorado. To tell you the truth, I've always believed in God, and have loved God, but I never listened to or followed Him. I recall knowing who He is. Now, I'm here in Adams County. When I first got here last year, I was nervous because I had been locked up in a different state. I thought it would be like that: I'd be alone, and I would get beat up and robbed, like in other jails.

But after awhile, I noticed how much calmer it is here. You see, in other states even though it's county jail, you have prison gangs, and the gangs run the show. I quickly noticed it was different here. After I got classified, they sent me to a minimum pod. I was like, "All right!" When I got there it had two TVs, a microwave, a hot water pot, and a soda machine. I was like, "Where am I, a Holiday Inn? Where is my continental breakfast?" As time went by, I would see people in prayer groups, reading the Bible, and going to worship. I would sit there, laugh, and make fun of those people.

Then one time, the Bible study leader asked me to join in. I said, "No. I have no weaknesses. I ain't weak like you." I did not want to join in, because going to church and praying shows a weakness to my gang and other inmates in Texas. I didn't want to get beat up or anything by other inmates who saw the weakness.

Well, I became a trustee, and I became the chaplain's assistant. I never went to church, or read the Bible, until I got this position. What really made me read the Bible was Chaplain McDonald's "A 100 Day Prayer Commitment." Since then, I've been working on getting closer to God. I especially want to thank Jesse Castro, and Mr. Richard Schmittal for inspiring me to become a Christian and to write this testimony. They opened my eyes to see that God can bring peace to jail.

26. SORRY SATAN, NICE TRY — Herman Perez

A week ago, I got a visit from my girlfriend and her mother. My girlfriend was crying along with her mom. I knew something was wrong. When I asked what happened, she told me that her brother beat her up. At the time, I was angry and was cursing at him, saying, "Why God? I'm not there to protect her. Please send one of your guardian angels to protect her."

After my visit which ended at 3:20 p.m., I went to my room with frustration and anger. I had tears in my eyes. My anger was getting the best of me. I was thinking what to do, who to call, or who to write. My heartbeat was going more than normal, so I got on my knees and prayed to God.

When I got done praying, I opened the Bible and it opened to Matthew. As I scanned through it, I found *Matthew 5:44*. It reads, *"But I tell you, love your enemies and pray for those who persecute you."*

That was what God wanted for me to read. Praise God! As I read a little more, I found another verse that fitted me at the time: *"For if you forgive men when they sin against you, your heavenly Father will also forgive you. (Matthew 6:14)*

A short time after that, they had cleared count at 3:55 p.m. Normally, they clear count, let us out of the room by 3:00 p.m., and our worship starts at 3:00 p.m. I believe God wanted me to calm down before they called Chaplains Worship. Sorry Satan, nice try! It shows you three important things to remember: Love, faith and hope. Without love for God, or for my girlfriend's brother, I would have lost it. I probably would have done something that I would have regretted. Without the work of faith, and labor of love, and patience of hope in our

Lord Jesus Christ, I probably wouldn't be here today to finish up my testimony. Like I said, "Sorry Satan, nice try!"

27. GOD HELD ME TO MY PROMISE — Mike Fisher, Volunteer at ACDF

One Sunday morning I woke up and couldn't breathe. After what seemed like an eternity at the hospital emergency room, the doctor informed me that my lung had collapsed. This wasn't good news for me because an aunt had had the same symptoms; she died of lung cancer two months after the diagnosis.

I hadn't been to church for a while, but I remembered how to pray. I made deals with God all morning. I told him I would do anything if he would just be with me. Well, first of all, you aren't supposed to make deals with God, and I knew that. But when you're scared, you grab at anything.

The doctor told me he had looked at the x-rays and didn't see any signs of cancer. That was the biggest sigh of relief I had ever felt. Things weren't all roses though: the lung wouldn't heal. After a week in the hospital, surgery was required to sew up the weak places on my lungs. This was supposed to be a simple procedure. I would be out of the hospital in three to four days. During the surgery, the right lung decided to take a vacation while the doctor was working on the left one. Thirty minutes later, they had me breathing again, but that was excessively long to go without oxygen.

I was in intensive care for several days. The only thing I remember about intensive care, was the doctor telling me what had happened during surgery and that I might have severe brain damage. So it was back to praying. Again, I told God I would do anything he wanted me to if He would just be with me. After three weeks, I was released from the hospital. The doctor told me when he released me that if I weren't a Christian, I might want to look into it, and if I was, I should go to church and thank God that I was okay. "By all the laws of medical science you shouldn't be alive. And, since you are alive, you should have the mentality of a five year old." Those were his exact words, and I will never forget them.

We started going to church, and a few months later during a church service, the Holy Spirit did a number on my wife; I was led to volunteering with community corrections. I started working with the homeless who were also drug addicts or alcoholics. I got the hardcore alcoholics, one of whom hadn't breathed a sober breath in a year. During the four years I worked with the homeless, I learned that these people are searching for something, but many don't know what it is, so they grab at anything. I also learned from visiting them in jails, rehab facilities, and hospitals that they are in need of some compassion and unconditional love. At one rehab facility, there were only two on-staff that the patients had respect for; they were both recovering alcoholics, and could sympathize with them.

A few years later, I got into prison ministry and discovered a whole new ministry. Later, I received a call from our pastor; Chaplain McDonald had asked her about people to volunteer for the Adams County Detention Facility. Since then, there are three of us from Fort Lupton United Methodist Church who lead Bible Study on Thursday night every week. My wife and I lead worship three Friday nights a month. All three of us feel this is the most fulfilling thing we have done in our service to God. We receive as much from Bible study as our friends do. The Holy Spirit is in that place. You can feel Him when you walk in the front door.

This passage always comes to mind when I talk to people about prison ministry. Jesus said, *"I was in prison and you came to visit me...I tell you the truth, whatever you did for one of the least of these brothers of mine, you did for me." (Matthew 25:36b-40b)* This should be our mission statement in all our service to God. God held me to my promise: that I would do anything He wanted me to do if He would be with me, and He has blessed me greatly with this jail ministry.

28. WALK THROUGH MY LIFE — Fran Saxon, Volunteer

I grew up in a lower class of people. Because of this, I would walk many bends and forks on the road of life. In my house, there were nine brothers and sisters along with my mom and dad. Mom was a stay-at-home mom without much education. My father worked all of the time, sometimes up to three jobs, to make ends meet. Our home was located in a part of town that was considered the "wrong side of the tracks."

When I was about to start school, I was stricken with an illness that almost took my life. I did not know what was happening to me. I remember mom crying and dad saying we just have to get the doctor here. I remember lying in my parents' bed and closing my eyes. I suddenly noticed a light that grew brighter and brighter. I heard someone say, "Open your eyes, Frances, and follow your heart." I can remember that because my mom said, "The Lord was with you and gave you back to us." Because of my age, I did not understand at all. I just knew that I was to do something to help others.

Later on in my life, I became acquainted with a lady who was much older than I was, and she had been very hurt. She had burns over her entire body from having been struck by lightning. Even though she was in such pain, I could see in her eyes that she was a very caring person. She would call me over and give me a penny or a nickel, and say, "Spend it: give some to others, and some to yourself." I found I could confide in her, and she would comfort me with her stories. One day, my oldest brother tried to rape me, and I told her what had happened. She said, "Follow your heart, dear Fran, and don't let this fill your heart with hate." I began to understand what God had told me back when I was so young — that I need to fill my heart with love and follow it.

Even though things were going well, I still was that person with not so good clothes: who walked to school with holes in her shoes, but I knew God was with me. I also knew that it would not last long. I had this sister who would always beat me, hurt me very badly, and call me names. If I did not do what she told me, she threatened me with serious physical harm. One day, she hurt me so badly that I took a knife and was going to hurt her just as badly. But, this voice in my head and heart said, "Frances, follow your heart." I threw down the knife and ran out of the house.

I walked for miles that day until I was about forty miles from my home. Even though I was scared, I was not going to return home. I kept praying "Dear God, I want to be good, and I want to be someone." Again this voice would say, "Frances, follow your heart." Later, I called home and told them what had happened, and where I was. One of my older sisters took me in for awhile. Then, much to my delight, my aunt and uncle kept me until my aunt from California invited me to spend the summer with them.

Once again, life was good, and I was very happy in California. However, one day tragedy struck. My aunt and I were driving into town, and we stumbled on what is now the famous "Watts Riots," in Los Angeles. A group of black persons forced our car to stop. My aunt was pulled out, and was beaten to death in front of me. Upon my return home, I found myself bitter and hateful toward all black people, because of what happened to my aunt.

One day, when I was working at a hospital, I was asked to help this burn patient. I looked in her room and saw that she was black. I immediately refused to enter the room, but the sister (this was a Catholic hospital) told me I must face what had happened to me. I did what I was told, and in time, I got to know this patient better. I even found myself helping her often and visiting her frequently. One day, she asked for some water, took a drink, and then said something very curious that was totally out of the blue. She told me that things would be better for me one day only if I would open and follow my heart. Later that night, she died. I will never forget her, for she made me open my heart once again. I started to follow my heart by working with people, and help those that others would not.

In March of 2005, I was asked to be part of the

"Transformation Project for Prison Ministry," from one of my Pastors. I was a little nervous about becoming involved in prison ministry, and frightened of the prospect actually going to a prison facility. I didn't give an answer right away, so he gave me plenty of time to think about it. Later one Sunday, I saw a woman sitting at a table all by her self so I decided to introduce myself to her. Her name was Rev. Yong Hui McDonald. She asked me to sit down and talk with her. She was with the Transformation Project. After our discussion, she invited me to come to Adams County Detention Facility, and give my testimony to the inmates. She told me that my story would help bring hope to those who are caught in a hopeless place. At the end of the conversation, I told her I would come and sing some songs: that I would think about telling my testimony. I had already decided that my story was too personal, to ever be told to strangers. Then, I read her book *Journey with Jesus* and my eyes were opened. I realized that the events of my past, although painful and difficult to talk about, were events that shaped my spiritual being, and moved me closer to Jesus. I suddenly realized that I was one of those teens that could have easily gone down the wrong path, if it had not been for the love and support of others, that kept me on the right path and out of trouble.

Her book made me realize that we all have something inside that holds us captive, and that the first step toward freedom of that captivity, is to share it with others—no matter how difficult the story. I fully embraced the challenge by Rev. McDonald by joining her at the prison to sing, and tell my story. It was truly inspiring to others, as she said it would be. It gave me the confidence in the fact that my life has meaning, and Jesus is using me as his instrument to spread His work and ministry. My heart was opened to knowing that if they find Jesus the way I found Him, that their lives would also be put on the right path.

Rev. McDonald has encouraged me to come out of my "comfort zone," and help bring hope and joy to those in jail. To look past the circumstances that brought them there, and deliver into their soul by discovering the good that is still there. To give them hope that Jesus loves them and has a plan for their lives. I've had my ups and downs, with all kinds of things happening to me, and to others I love. I have seen a friend grief-stricken after she was told her son was brutally murdered by his lover. Another time, I found myself comforting a friend whose daughter was killed at the hands of a young boy that I knew from the school where I worked. I have seen my church give me love and then take it back. I know that God is always near and that I still have to walk the path He has chosen for me. I have learned to hold my head up, to cry with those and pray for those who I see walking down that wrong path.

29. WEEPING FOR JOY — Rev. Alan Marquez, Volunteer

I accepted Jesus Christ as my Lord and Savior while serving in the US Army on Okinawa, Japan. Raised in a non-Christian home, I lived a godless and sinful life of violence, immorality and drug abuse. While in Okinawa, I often frequented a location known as "BC Street" which was known for its wild entertainment with prostitutes and bars.

One night while on BC Street, I was handed a pamphlet by a Christian, that spoke to me about Jesus Christ and my relationship with Him. I took this track back to the barracks, and for the first time in my life, I read the Word of God. I became aware of my need to be born again.

"In reply Jesus declared, "I tell you the truth, no one can see the kingdom of God unless he is born again." (John 3:3) Some time later, I prayed and accepted Jesus as my personal Savior. He not only forgave my sins, but He delivered me from my bondage to a very evil lifestyle. I was and will forever be grateful to the Lord for this!

Having been exposed to the "Good News" of Jesus outside of a church building, I made a commitment never to forget those still on the street (outside of the Church services). For over thirty-four years, this commitment has taken me almost around the world. I have shared Jesus with thousands: in hospitals, nursing homes, homeless shelters, marketplaces, on city streets, and in jails, and prisons. Many have been saved, and I have experienced the spirit of God doing great things. However, I have never experienced the manifestations of God's Spirit, and of God's great love, anywhere else as I have in jails and prisons. I have seen prisoners transformed in a week's time. I didn't recognize them from the week before. I have seen men and women delivered from demonic activities in their lives. Hope and purpose restored to the destitute, relationships restored with loved ones, and men and women who once lived destructive, self-centered lives become productive and caring citizens.

The joy and fulfillment I have experienced as a volunteer clergy working among incarcerated men and women cannot be expressed. I have been so deeply moved that, at times, it has been difficult for me to speak without weeping for days after participating in services where Christ revealed Himself to both inmates and volunteers in a wonderful and powerful way. If other Christians knew of this blessed, fruitful, and rewarding ministry, they would rush out to ACDF and other correctional facilities: to share in the joy of bringing the "Good News" of the Lord Jesus Christ to these spiritually hungry men and women.

As it is written in *Isaiah 52:7*, "*How beautiful on the mountains are the feet of those who bring good news, who proclaim peace, who bring good tidings, who proclaim salvation.....*" And in *Matthew 25:36b-40; "I was in prison and you came to visit me....I will tell you the truth, whatever you did for one of the least of these brothers of mine, you did for me.*" It is my prayer that those reading this testimony will sincerely pray and ask the Lord if He would have them participate in Christian ministry to the many men and women incarcerated in jails and prisons around the world.

30. DISCOVERY OF THE MAXIMUM SAINTS
— Chaplain McDonald

One of the most touching stories that came out of the book *Maximum Saints Never Hide in the Dark,* is a story of a young man Jason Vigil. When Jason shared with me how this book changed his life because Marla accepted Christ before she passed away, I was so encouraged. I said to myself, "Many people worked hard for this book, and if all the hard work was done only for Jason, it was worth it." I also remember Rosemae, who introduced Jesus to Marla. Rosemae and Michah Collins were leading Bible study in their own pods. They both were powerful leaders and mentoring many people. Praise God for these Maximum Saints!

Another story I will share here is something I will never forget, how maximum saints are making a difference in our facility. When I was gathering people for Chaplain's Worship on Saturday, July 1, 2006., from F Module, there was a verbal altercation between two people on the second floor. The control tower deputy called for a deputy and in the mean time, I saw something I had never seen in the midst of turmoil. Suddenly, all of the men formed a big circle holding hands and praying the Lord's prayer. About midway through the prayer, the deputy from F2300 came out. When the prayer was over, everyone was calm, and ready to go to worship. I told the deputy that if I had any problems at the service, I would call him. The worship service went fine.

The next day, I visited the man who was shouting on that day of service. I told him how upset I was by his actions, how violent words or actions wouldn't bring any good results, but cause a destructive ripple effect for many people. After I explained my views on how to resolve the conflict, he agreed with what I had said, and told me that he would do better, by trying his hardest so this wouldn't happen again.

I also visited F2200 to thank the two leaders who suggested to the others to hold hands and pray. I asked the leaders to prepare a sermon on how to resolve conflicts peacefully. The following week, during the Chaplain's Worship Service, the man who had done the shouting apologized to the other man, and to the whole group. Then, Lloyd Henderson, one of the leaders from F2200 preached about how God helped them to have a peaceful resolution to avoid conflict through prayer. Maximum Saints worked overtime that day.

Many great things are happening in our facility because of these Maximum Saints in our facility. I have a vision for these Maximum Saints when they leave the facility. Someday, I hope it will be soon, I would like to see some of the *Maximum Saints* stories made into a movie to tell the world that God can use people mightily even if they made grave mistakes.

Also, the many Maximum Saints from ACDF as musical performers and speakers at the Pepsi Center in Denver, Colorado, to tell the world that God can use anyone when they are willing to pay the price and follow Jesus.

In addition, I would like to see many Maximum Saints arise from the "family of the incarcerated" as well. If one person out of each incarcerated family would be involved in prison ministry, we would have at least 30,000 people involved in prison ministry in Colorado.

Many are going through so much pain and suffering because they are affected by incarceration, especially innocent children. I challenge everyone who reads this to reach out to others who are hurting, not only incarcerated, but also incarcerated families, and hurting children. We have the responsibility to take care of hurting people. May God bless you.

Part Two:
Sermons & Meditations

Drawing "Praying Saints" by Charles Polk

31. THOSE WHO SEEK THE LORD IN THE 11TH HOUR, DUE AT 10:30 — Thomas Golden

#1. What is life? #2. Who am I? #3. When will all this end? #4. What is it I'm expected to do with my life? We experience a lot of "firsts" in our lives: first kiss, first car, first love, and so on. I had a "first" last night guys, that is totally out of the picture for me. I've cried more in these last few months than I have in all my life, all selfish tears. "Why this? Why that?" You get the picture? "Why me, Lord?"

Last night, the tears fell once again, but this time they weren't for me. I looked around me. I saw young men whose lives are in total disarray and destruction, because of drugs, alcohol, and yes, sin. Some might not ever see freedom again. I saw the guys like myself, who have way more years behind them than they have left, all caught up in this whirlwind of death. The tears last night were for all of you: your pain, your confusion, and your lost potential in life. I find that so sad, and I've never cared about anything, not even myself.

What is life? Life is a gift from God. In *Jeremiah 1:5*, God says He knew you before He formed you in your mother's womb, and He makes the same statement in *Psalms 139*. In these chapters He answers question #2, "Who am I?"at least for those who are in Christ. Who are you? Are you tired? Are you looking for someone (or something in life), but can't seem to find it? For me, it's Christ! I challenge you, is He what you are looking for?

Before I go any further, I would like to share the story of a man whose lot in life was to feel all alone, even when surrounded by those who loved him. He was caught up in drugs, alcohol and nothingness, plus he was married to a woman he knew he had never loved. So, he hugged his little boy, telling him he was sorry, but that he had to go. He walked away with that sound of his sins, and tears, hardening his heart. He was running away with his fears. The boy was fourteen years old. Twelve years passed. Now the little boy is a young man twenty-six years old, with a four year old boy of his own.

The father found God and is in the process of change. One more prison sentence and another marriage are in the act. He asks his son from his first marriage to be his best man at his third attempt at love. The young boy, now a man, looks at his father and says he's been proud of him all his life as he watched his father struggle with drug addiction, and now is free.

"God" was the father's answer. The boy calmly states, "I don't need God. You left me when I was fourteen, and all I have, I got myself." The young man was making about $60,000 a year, flying from Oregon, to Nevada, to California, working for a big construction company. He didn't use drugs and very seldom drank. He was all around a pretty good guy. The father didn't push God at his son. After all, he was only twenty-six, and he still had his whole life ahead of him. Right?

Heaven or hell, life or death—those are the choices regardless of whether we believe. Jesus states that even if a man gains the whole world and loses his own soul, he is lost. Hebrews, in chapter two, tells us to stay alert so as not to slip away. *2 Corinthians 6:2b* says, *"Now is the time of God's favor, now is the day of salvation."*

Proverbs 27:1 tells you not to boast about tomorrow for none of us know what tomorrow will bring. The young man I was talking about died two weeks after his father and he had this conversation. It reminds me of *Proverbs 29:1* which says, *"A man who remains stiff-necked after many rebukes will suddenly be destroyed-- without remedy."*

Question #3 is, "When will all this end?" Death will bring an end to your chances of life. Do you know how many years you get to live? Consider the statement Jesus made. He said, "I will come as a thief in the night." I hear guys say, "I know God, and He already knows my sins, and He will forgive me" Jesus said, *"Not everyone who says to me, 'Lord, Lord,' will enter the kingdom of heaven, but only he who does the will of my Father who is in heaven. Many will say to me on that day, 'Lord, Lord, did we not prophesy in your name, and in your name drive out demons and perform many miracles?' Then I will tell them plainly, 'I*

never knew you. Away from me, you evildoers!'" (Matthew 7:21-23)
Does your sin bring you so much pleasure that you are willing
to gamble? He knows your heart. You cannot justify or excuse
sin away. In his eyes, you are either seeking Him or following
the flesh.

#4 "What is it I'm expected to do with my life?" I'll tell
you. You are to take the Word of God, preaching and teaching
to all nations to the ends of the earth. Can you be caught in your
sin and still go to heaven? I'll let you answer that, but this is
what the Lord says: we are to become like Christ, and in our
Christian walk we are to be careful not to lead someone astray
by our actions. I asked what a man can take to heaven when he
dies. Do you know? Ask yourself, out of all you have or can get
in the future, what can you take with you?

The only thing you can take with you is your character,
and that is revealed in your relationships with family, friends
and others brought into your life. Stop and ask yourself, "Does
my action reveal our Father in heaven?" There is a song about a
father wanting to be a shining example to his son because the
only Father is in heaven. What he should see is the Father living
within him. Please, don't let your loved ones down. That young
man I was talking about was my son Jeremy. I let him down.
Yes, my Father loves him more than I ever could. I pray that He
gave him one more chance, but I am not sure. I can't say
anything about your walk, but I let my baby down. I won't let
down someone else's baby.

Life is short. Let your light shine to the world. Share
every chance you get because I don't know what it is going to
be like to walk the streets of gold in heaven if my son isn't there
to walk with me. No one but you can make the choice to live for
God forever, but we can teach the ones we love of the One who
is love. Teach and guide your children in the ways of the Lord,
and when they grow up, they won't stray. If you noticed, I
value the Scriptures for one reason: you decide where you, and
maybe your children, want to spend eternity.

I will end with this from Romans. Paul says he would

gladly give up his right for heaven for his brothers. (Romans 9:1 -3) I would give up my soul if it would help the ones I love, but it won't. Only your walk and Christ living in you can make a difference. Study His Word so that you can do the good deeds he has set up for you. Make your choice. Don't wait.

32. I AM THE VINE — Steven Rodriguez

Read *John 15:1-8.* Jesus is speaking in verse 5, *"I am the vine; you are the branches. If a man remains in me and in him, he will bear much fruit; apart from me you can do nothing."*

The first thing to learn is what fruit meant. It is the fruit of the Spirit according to the Apostle Paul in *Galatians 5:22: "But the fruit of the Spirit is love, joy, peace, patience, kindness, goodness, faithfulness, gentleness and self-control. Against such things there is no law."* God's power produces these fruits in our lives when we give every part of our lives over to Him and trust in Him to take care of us. He expects each of us to put all our trust in Him. That's what Jesus means for us to remain in Him, and He will remain in us. That's what provides the right nutrients for us to have the fruit of the Spirit.

In all my years of being lost in sin, I always felt like those "fruits" were too good to be true and too good for me. I knew what love was, and at times I felt love for other people, my family, and my children, but for many years I didn't feel loved. Love is very important to us. That might be why love is key in the "first and greatest" command of Jesus (*Matthew 22:38*). The second command and just as important is based on love also, *love for God first love for our neighbors second. Matthew 22:40* states, *"All the Law and the Prophets hang on these two commandments."* By Jesus saying this, I believe that love is vital to all other "fruits." Joy, kindness, peace, all of it can't be alive in us if we are without love.

I was like the branch "useless and withered" with no fruits. I feel like I was just about to be cut off and burned up with all the rest of the dead branches. I was spiritually dead, living for my selfish desires, seeking to please only my fleshly needs. My connection was with the devil and all the lies he would put in my head. Satan had me believing that if God was real, He didn't want anything to do with me. How could God love me on the other side of all the hurtful events in my life? I didn't understand the way God does things and Satan used my ignorance to plant seeds for his rotten fruits, anger, fear, bitterness, pain, and so on.

My heart grew hard and I was a very corrupt person and I went for every line Satan had, hook, line and sinker. Remember, I was a "dirty rotten scoundrel." In me was Satan's recipe for a dirty rotten fruit pie. That's a very painful way to live. I would wake up and all the world was a dark cloud of ugliness and I used that to feed and justify my feelings of anger, guilt, disappointment and such. I was being burned from the inside out and only trying to get used to the heat instead of searching for a way to put the fire out. It took a long time but God has shown me the truth about His love for me.

(1) I am created by God in His image, so I am not a dirty rotten scoundrel.

(2) God wants everything to do with me. He wants to be my source of all good things in my life.

(3) God loves me and it's His will for me to be able to enjoy the fruits of His Spirit. Not just for right now but for all of eternity.

(4) God is God of truth and His word gives us His truth so we can combat against the lies of Satan.

I now am like the branches "pruned and purified." I'm just starting but I know God's Spirit is at work to produce fruit through me. The amount of fruit is endless, and God has the power to give as much in the area He wants. He knows what is best for us. We just have to put 100% of our trust in Him and His ways even if we don't understand His way very much. We're in a war and in order for us to have any fruit of the Spirit, we need to walk in, think in, sleep in, do everything we do in Jesus. Remember Jesus said, "apart from me, you can do nothing." In order for us to be fruitful, we need to stay attached.

33. WHAT MASTER DO YOU CHOOSE TO SERVE
— Alan Taylor

From 1995 up until August 2001, I had been through numerous drug and alcohol classes, along with any other class the state of Colorado deemed necessary. It wasn't until I sincerely asked the Lord into my heart and began to thoroughly search the Scriptures to prove myself true that I had the real spiritual awakening that I needed. As in *James 1:5-8*, I asked God, I didn't doubt, and I began a spiritual journey. I was literally sent to Bible school via the Department of Corrections. I have been clean and sober since August of 2001. God did the same for my wife, and she has been clean and sober since June 2002.

Drugs, when used for other than the medical purpose that society has regulated them for, are means by which Satan is able to enter the body. Even in our fairy tales, such as the one about Sleeping Beauty, a witch or sorceress, makes a "magical" brew that is placed in an apple, and when eaten, causes Sleeping Beauty to fall asleep. It is the same with those of us who manufacture meth, rock up powder cocaine, or cook up heroin; we are merely modern day witches and sorcerers that aid Satan and his demonic nymphs in destroying ourselves and our brothers and sisters. There is a whole lot more to my story. After all, I said I had that habit for twenty-five years, but I'm saving that for my book and possibly, by God's will, a movie.

As we go through life, I would like you, as children of God, to remember this, "The devil truly is dope." As a 1970s O'Jay's song once phrased, and God said, "You cannot serve two masters; you will surely hate one and love the other." What master do you choose to serve?

34. IT DOESN'T MATTER WHAT YOU HAVE DONE, GOD WILL FORGIVE YOU — Samuel Uribe

I first gave my life to Jesus when I was nine or ten years old. My dad had just gotten out of prison and was really into the Lord. I remember him telling me about a man named Jesus and how He died for me, so when I die, I can go to heaven to be with Him forever. That day, we got on our knees and said a prayer, "The Sinner's Prayer." At the time, I really didn't understand everything, but I trusted my dad, and in my little heart, I knew it was true.

I soon figured out that God, Jesus and the devil were just a story my dad made up so I would be a good little boy, and I was good until I turned fourteen. I started smoking weed and drinking. At sixteen, I joined a gang and dropped out of school. By that time, I was sniffing cocaine, stealing cars, robbing houses and people, and committing many other crimes. For some reason, I just didn't care. I thought I was "bad." I never had the "finer things in life," but I wanted them. Then, I started trippin' acid. At first it was fun, but it soon took me to a dark, evil place, and I liked it, especially when I would see "demons."

One night, at a party while I was trippin' acid, I walked out to the alley. I called on Satan. I said, "If you are real, show yourself." Next thing you know "A man" appeared. He said he was Satan himself, and he had been watching and me and he liked what he saw. He told me, "You are a soldier. I want your star." It was like he could read my mind when he asked, "Which car do you want?" Suddenly, across the street five cars appeared that weren't there before. He then asked, "You want girls, how many?" Out of nowhere, all these girls came running out of the apartment complex across the street. At the same time, the street became filled with police cars, lights and sirens blaring. "The man" snapped his fingers, and they vanished instantly. He smiled and said, "See, I am the Prince of Darkness. What? You still don't believe?" I replied, "I didn't. I need a cigarette, make a pack of cigarettes appear." He said, "It doesn't work that way." He then took the forty ounce bottle of beer I was drinking out of my hand, tapped the top of it with his hand and gave it back to me full and unopened.

This amazed and scared me because the bottle had been almost empty. He told me, "God don't love you. If he did, he would give you what you want. Why do you suffer? But I love you. I'll give you whatever you want. All you have to do is give me your star and fight with me at the final battle. If you sell me your soul, you'll live until that day, plus I'll make you rich, give you the finest women, and everyone will fear you." He pulled out a scroll and cut his hand; he told me to cut mine and to sign it in blood.

I got this bad feeling that if I signed he would kill me. I said, "No, you are tricking me!" He became very angry and started cussing at me, "Who do you think you are? Do you think I just go around showing myself to everyone?" He punched me in the chest and nearly knocked me out. He picked me up and said, "Sorry. But you don't seem to understand who you are dealing with. I just want to show you the power. I love you. Let my spirit be your spirit. I know you are not ready yet, but you'll be back. When you are ready, write down what you want and sign it in your blood. Then, pray to me like you would God."

By this time, I was freaked out. I turned and started running. About two blocks down, he popped out of a bus shelter and said, "If you ever tell anyone about this, I'll kill you!" My grandma's house was close by. I went there. I was crying when my auntie let me in. I told her everything. My auntie and my cousin began reading from the Bible about Jesus' death and resurrection. I started screaming like I was possessed when I heard the name Jesus. It made my whole body hurt. It felt like something was inside of me punching my stomach. After twenty minutes, or so, I calmed down. Then, my mom came in. She was mad. She said, "Someone just did a drive-by shooting on our house." Then, I remembered what the devil told me. "If you tell anyone, I'll kill you!"

A few weeks later, out of fear and greed, I made a contract with Satan and signed it in blood. I also began praying to him. This happened when I was seventeen years old. A few weeks after that, I met "A man" at a party who said he had twenty pounds of marijuana for me. I didn't even know him, but he said I was going to be his new partner. Soon, I was also selling cocaine, acid, and guns. This went on for about two years. During that time, I began dabbling in witchcraft, black magic, tarot cards, and read the Necronomican and the Satanic Bible while communicating with Satan through the Ouija board. I became very violent and obsessed with death. I believed I was a demon who could not die. There were many times I should have, including numerous car wrecks and shoot-outs, that only strengthened this belief.

One night, a friend came over to my house. His girlfriend showed up and they began arguing. He put the gun to his head and said, "Tonight, I'll meet the devil. Look!" and blew his head in half. That night, I realized life was precious and the way I was living was wrong. I wanted out of that contract with Satan, but I felt trapped. I didn't change my ways, and as of today, there are twenty-seven convictions on my police record.

In November 2001, I had just turned twenty-three years old when my first daughter was born. As I held her and looked into her eyes, I felt a love I never felt before. Because of her, I became less violent, but I still did a lot of the same things although she was the most important thing in my life and came first over my friends and myself. A couple months after she was born, I was walking downtown when someone shot at me. I hit the ground and when I got up a man was standing there. He just handed me a tract. Usually, when someone would do this, I would throw it away. This time, I read it. In big letters it said, "Did you know Jesus has the power to rip up that contract you signed with Satan?" Inside, it said that no matter what I've done, even if I killed somebody, God would forgive me because of what Jesus did on the Cross. It said that, if I admit I'm a sinner and ask for forgiveness, God would forgive my past.

I still wasn't so sure. That same night, my step-dad asked me, "Do you know children are a gift from God?" I knew God was trying to talk to me. I can't say if it was that night but it was soon afterwards when God did talk to me! I was sleeping when something lifted me up, "Wake up!" I knew it was God. I didn't hear a voice, but He was speaking to my heart. He asked, "Why are you running from me?" "God, is that you?" I cried, shaking uncontrollably. I was scared, but then an overwhelming sense of peace came over me, and I couldn't stop crying. "Yes," He answered, "Stop running from me! I do love you and want to show you the truth. Do you really think Satan loves you? He hates you. He hates you because you belong to me. (I remembered my dad's words.) Do you think it was him that saved your life all those times? (Flashbacks of all the times I should have died went through my head.) It was me! I knew you before you were born. I don't hate you. The devil is a liar. I love you more than you can ever imagine. I have plans for you, to give you a good life, but only if you let me." "Where have you been?" I asked. He replied, "Everyday I knock at your door, but you never let me in. Only if you allow me in will I be able to reveal the truth to you. Can I come in?" "Yes," I cried. "Please show me because I'm lost, and I don't know what to do."

God told me if I confess my sins and repent and believe Jesus died for me, I would have the free gift of life. If not, I would die soon, and it was His will that none should perish but all shall live. He said the deal I made with Satan had no power and tonight salvation was being offered. This was a new contract that was unbreakable and indestructible which no man on earth or no demon in hell can ever destroy and that this was possible only because (he stressed this point very much) and only because of the blood of Jesus. Because His Son Jesus was the ultimate sacrifice, He died for the sins of the world, and the battle was won on the Cross. He said the only way to the Father was through the Son. He told me to read His Word and keep it, that His Spirit was my spirit; that my body is His temple and to keep it clean. The old me is dead and He would give me a new heart, the heart of Christ. I confessed my sins and asked for forgiveness. I told Him I've always believed and was sorry.

The next day I couldn't stop crying. My Mom said the change in me was like night and day. I couldn't stop reading the Bible and finally felt free. I began going to church and telling everyone I knew about Jesus. Most people, especially my friends, laughed at me. A lot of people turned their backs on me, even family. I got made fun of a lot, and it hurt. At church I would tell people my story. I was shunned, hardly anyone believed me. They said I was "on drugs" and "God don't come to people like that" I bounced around from church to church, never finding a "home" or feeling welcome. I was always "The New Guy" or "Just a baby Christian" or "The Stranger." I became discouraged. Soon, I stopped going to church altogether.

About a year after my experience with God, I began smoking weed and drinking occasionally. I still prayed daily and read the Bible, thinking God understands. He knows I'm weak. I take care of my responsibilities. Besides, I've come a long way compared to what I used to be, but "God's temple," my body, was not clean.

From November 2001 until recently, my relationship with God was lukewarm. I always prayed to Him and thanked Him for everything, but I was still living in sin. However, I managed to stay out of jail during that time, except for a D.U.I., which I did not even stay in jail more than a couple of days for because I was put on probation. But in the summer of 2005, I tried to work things out with my daughter's mom. She got pregnant, but we weren't faithful to each other. One night, she came at me with a knife, and I beat her up. I plead guilty to "attempted assault." I was sentenced to one year work release.

On May 1, 2006, I turned myself in. As I was being booked in, I was told I was denied work release by the jail. I felt God had a different plan for me. I said a prayer, "God, I know I've been going back to my old ways. I know I'm dirty. I know I can do nothing without you. I know I've put other things above you. Please make me clean. I need help. I can't do it on my own. I know you are in charge, and I trust you. Do what you have to do to make me the man you want me to be."

When I got to my pod, I read a couple of books but could never get into them. Then I picked up another book. The cover was missing. I turned to the middle and read. It was a story about a man who knew the Lord, fell away, came to jail and knows the Lord again. Only now, he really knows Him on a whole new level. This book had other stories of pain, struggle, survival and most importantly, victory, victory through Christ. The name of that book is *Maximum Saints Never Hide in the Dark* It gave me the encouragement to live for Christ. I mean really live, not just fifty per cent but one hundred per cent. It made me realize that I have to surrender to Christ to really know Him, just like when I turned myself in. I surrendered.

I now know in order for me to really know Jesus, I must be willing to deny myself all the fleshly things of this world. Things really aren't important. Just as God sacrificed His only Son, I also must make a sacrifice — myself! God's Word says, "You will find me when you seek me with all your heart." I want to find God. I want that relationship. I remember before I just wanted His blessings, but now, I just want Him. Without Him, everything else is meaningless! Remember, it doesn't matter what you've done. Our Lord will forgive you because of what Jesus did on the Cross. The devil is a liar! Jesus is the Truth, the Light, and the Way. The only Way! *"Therefore, I urge you, brothers, in view of God's mercy, to offer your bodies as living sacrifices, holy and pleasing to God – this is your spiritual act of worship. Do not conform any longer to the pattern of this world, but be transformed by the renewing of your mind. Then you will be able to test and approve what God's will is – his good, pleasing and perfect will." (Romans 12:1-2)*

35. GOD'S WILL — Richard Schmittal

Is it WRONG to want the good things in life? Doesn't Scripture tell us to seek first the kingdom of heaven and all these other things shall be added unto you? The real key to the good things in life has to do with what God views as good and His expression of that goodness toward us.

Scripture tells us: *"Every good and perfect gift is from above, coming down from the Father of the heavenly lights." (James 1:17a)*

So we know God is the source, but we must ask, what are the good things in life? God is good. That is to say, His very nature is good. Therefore, His desire is to express every form of goodness possible to His children. He made the ultimate expression of that goodness as *Romans 8:32* tell us, *"He who did not spare his own Son, but gave him up for us all-how will he not also, along with him, graciously give us all things?"*

Christ's sacrifice for our sin, and for the sins of all who would believe, was the demonstration of His pure love for us. However, when the crucifixion took place, it did not appear to be a positive thing. In fact, Jesus Himself prayed that, if possible, *"My Father, if it is possible, may this cup be taken from me. Yet not as I will, but as you will." (Matthew 26:39b)*

It's hard to see hardships in a positive manner. Most people would define life's good things as whatever makes us happy. However, we don't see from God's point of view. We tend to judge situations by how they affect us right now. What we fail to see is that some of the Lord's greatest blessings come in situations that, at the time, cause us the most pain. God takes our seemingly terrible circumstances and works them to benefit us. (*Romans 8:28*)

The good things in life then, are all things that fit into God's plan and purpose for our lives, though we don't understand at the time why God would allow certain trials in our lives. Think of Joseph; he was sold as a slave, thrown into a pit, confused and overwhelmed. But later, Joseph learned God meant it for good. I think the most important thing is to stay focused on Christ through these hardships. *"You will keep in perfect peace him whose mind is steadfast, because he trusts in you." (Isaiah 26:3)*

Though keeping our mind on things above is difficult when we are hurting, when we do, our Lord and Savior Jesus Christ will always make this known to us – *"No temptation has seized you except what is common to man. And God is faithful; he will not let you be tempted beyond what you can bear." (1 Corinthians 10:13a)* That's how we can make it through worldly hardships.

We must keep saying, "God, I know your promises and all you have done in my life. So, I am trusting you." I don't always feel like it, and there are days I really don't like what is happening, but like Jesus, I must say, "God, not my will, but yours. God, I trust you."

We must hold onto God's promises when we face difficulties in our lives. We must trust that things will get better; we must choose at those times when we are at our lowest to lean on God's loving promises. *"For I know the plans I have for you, declares the Lord. Plans to prosper you and not to harm you; plans to give you hope and a future. Then you will call upon me and come and pray to me and I will listen to you. You will seek me and find me when you seek me with all your heart." (Jeremiah 29:11-13)*

No suffering, hardship, or loneliness seems pleasant at the time, though we learn obedience from what we suffer. *"No discipline seems pleasant at the time, but painful. Later on, however, it produces a harvest of righteousness and peace for those who have been trained by it." (Hebrews 12:11)* In fact, we can and should rejoice when we go through trials. *"Not only so, but we also rejoice in our sufferings, because we know that suffering produces perseverance; perseverance, character; and character, hope. And hope does not disappoint us, because God has poured out his love into our hearts by the Holy Spirit whom he has given us." (Romans 5:3-5)*

When our faith gets tested, we grow stronger in our faith: *"Consider it pure joy, my brothers, whenever you face trials of many kinds, because you know that the testing of your faith develops perseverance. Perseverance must finish its work so that you may be mature and complete, not lacking anything." (James 1:2-4)* It's a blessing in disguise to go through trial: *"Blessed is the man who perseveres under trial." (James 1:12a)* We shouldn't be surprised when trials come: *"Dear Friend, do not be surprised at the painful trial you are suffering... But rejoice."(1 Peter 4:12-13a)* Trials come, not to turn us away from Christ, but to draw us closer to him, to bring us to repentance and to prayer: *"In this you greatly rejoice, though now for a little while you may have had to suffer grief in all kinds of trials."(1 Peter 1:6)*

God uses the situations in our lives to strengthen our faith, but he always rescues us: *"If this is so the Lord knows how to rescue godly men from trials and to hold the unrighteous for the Day of Judgment"* (2 Peter 2:9a) When we take the right attitudes in our trials, others see that we are worthy of God's kingdom: *"Therefore...we boast about your perseverance and faith in all the persecutions and trials you are enduring...and as a result you will be counted worthy of the kingdom of God, for which you are suffering."* (2 Thessalonians 1:4-5)

God has a path for your life, and if you will follow it that journey will change your life forever. We, as Christians, are called to trust God through the good times as well as the bad. Everything we face along the pathway is God's will for us. God knows ahead of time every turn in the road and travels with us until the journey's end which makes everything we've gone through worth it all: *"I consider that our present sufferings are not worth comparing with the glory that will be revealed in us."* (Romans 8:18)

I beg you to rely solely on Jesus Christ, our Lord. Let us look past these temporary troubles and wait patiently for Christ to deliver us from the storm. He knows all our needs before we ask. And when we have stood firm, He will bless us with the desires of our hearts. The Lord is with you. Always remember, what looks like a valley that we cannot get past. When viewed through our human eyes, is God at work in us — His blessings in disguise, God transforming our trials into triumphs! It's RIGHT to desire the good things in life when what we're seeking is what God says is good!

36. THE THREE THINGS — Linda Lovato

The three things I find myself struggling with: 1. doubt; 2. understanding of the Holy Spirit; 3. forgiving myself. Today I would like to tell you that I have finely realized and felt God's Holy Spirit in my life! I would like to tell you why my life has changed so much within such a short time.

I lost my second son, and I was a hater and angry with God for five years. I got involved with drugs, drinking and, to top it off, involved with a very controlling man. I got tired of my hateful, controlling, sad life. I was alive and reached out and prayed to God, "Please take me out of this chaotic life I have created." Four days later, I landed in jail for one hundred twenty days. During those one hundred twenty days here, I had a cellie who was God fearing and told me I needed to stop blaming God for what happened to my son.

At first I told her I wasn't blaming God, and then I realized I was, or I wouldn't have been angry and a hater for five years. I started having an open mind about everything in life. I asked God to forgive me and for the choices I had made in my life that have hurt my parents, siblings, sons and me I think about the sad, lost world I lived in for five years.

How I have hurt. To see my boys suffer because they're no longer with their mother because of my sorry actions tears me up inside. It makes me very angry at myself, and I'm having a hard time forgiving myself for my past actions. My nine year old son wrote to me in here saying he loves me with his heart, soul, and mind, and don't ever forget that. He wrote that he prays every day that his little brother and he will be back with me as a happy (as he calls it) family once again! So, I started thinking about what the chaplain tells us about how the Holy Spirit works in our lives. I realize how much I am loved and thought of every day by my loved ones, even though I let them down! This is God's way of showing me He loves me and forgives me through His Holy Spirit.

I can see and feel when He comforts me and helps me cope with the problems, hardships, loneliness, and just straight up struggles of life every day I am in here. He comforts my aching heart, every sorrow and every pain that I have gone through and am going through right now. I feel His loving arms hold me as I cry for His help, and He wipes my tears and tells me everything is going to be all right. I now realize how forgiving He is and that He is the one that makes all things, and without Him, we are nothing!

If He can forgive me, comfort me and make me laugh again in these times of struggle and loneliness, who am I to stop Him by not forgiving myself and letting Him take full control to heal me so I can make the right choices to be a good mother, daughter, sister, friend and child of God once again. My New Year's Resolution is to be forgiving in every possible way with those who have hurt me or are hurting me and, most of all, with myself. Then God's Holy Spirit can keep working in me to heal me, so I can live a happy family life once again. I find myself being grateful and thanking God for not giving up on me. But most of all, I want that little boy's prayer answered, and no doubt about it, I want to be healed! How about you?!

37. DON'T LET ANYTHING STOP YOU FROM SERVING THE LORD — Omar Castanada

When I served the devil, I sold drugs, and I was a tattoo artist and did body piercing for fifteen years. With all that, I was good. I also had an honest job, but at the same time I was using drugs to the point where we got kicked out of the first three apartments we had. I still didn't stop selling or using them. We ended up at my baby's mom's sister's apartment. There I ended up selling rock and taking control on that block. Nobody would sell there but me. This went on for a few years. I made a lot of money then, and we rented a house. Everything was good -- money, house, and family. In 2002, I got a drug charge. I did a deferred sentence, so there was no felony on that. I had a hard time because of selling and using drugs.

April 2004, is when I said, "Lord Jesus, I need you in my life." So, my walk with the Lord started when I decided to accept Jesus in my life. This was my thought. "I have been serving the devil for fifteen years. Now, I am going to serve God for fifteen years. When these fifteen years go by, I can decide which fifteen years were better, those serving the devil or those serving God."

I have a friend who gave me his number to call when I was ready, so I went to church with him. I tried to serve God but I got discouraged so I quit going. One day the Lord spoke to me when I was at home. "Why are you not going to church?" I said, "They just are bunch of hypocrites." He said, "You are there to hear my Words, not to judge the people." Still, I didn't go. This happened to me three times.

By October 1, I had lost my house, had lost my family, and had separated from my girlfriend of ten years. We have two daughters together, so she ended up with the little one and I kept the oldest. I lost all the things that we had — movies, CDs, entertainment center, cars, everything. I ended up with nothing but one daughter. Next thing you know, I was staying with my daughter's mom's sister again. Before that, I was in a car accident and ended up with a blood clot in my lung and three broken ribs. One morning, after I went to get my blood level checked and I took some pain pills, my baby's mom's sister was coming down the stairs. She told me that her sister's boyfriend beat her. I went to her apartment, and one thing led to another. I defended myself, and I got a murder charge.

God had a plan for me. I didn't see it. I ran to seek God's guidance. He showed me *2 Samuel 24:12-13*. I had to make a choice to either turn myself in or keep running away. God said, "You're going to preach my word the same way as when you were on the street selling drugs," I said, "My life is in your hands. Let it be so. I know I won't do this time alone, for you are with me." I turned myself in. The first day, I worried for my family. God told me not to worry, but to seek Him.

God spoke to me through the Scriptures. Jesus said, *"Anyone who loves his father or mother more than me is not worthy of me; anyone who loves his son or daughter more than me is not worthy of me; and anyone who does not take his cross and follow me is not worthy of me. Whoever finds his life will lose it, and whoever loses his life for my sake will find it. He who receives you receives me, and he who receives me receives the one who sent me."* (Matthew 10:37-40) "Wow!" I said to God, "Ok, I will trust you with everything that has to do with my family. You said you will be there. Your face I will seek, as the Psalmist said, and from now on, you are my number one in my life. I want to be worthy of you, and I will be devoted to you from now on." But like I said, I didn't know much about the Word of God. He said what is in *Isaiah 1:27-31*, powerful words of redemption by justice and destruction of those who forsake the Lord. All that I know I was taught by the Holy Spirit. I have been in jail and eight months in D.O.C., and I spread the word at D.R.D.C. cell house 5, and Crowley Correctional Facility.

One time, when I came from Crowley to Adams County jail on a writ, I was in the hole "writ pod," and there I got baptized by the Holy Spirit. I was given the gift of healing. At Crawley Correctional Facility, I healed three people by the Holy Spirit working through me, not for my glory but for the glory of God. Here I have healed two or three in the name of the Lord Jesus Christ. Read *Matthew 21:22: "If you believe, you will receive whatever you ask for in prayer,"* and my faith is so great, but all thanks to Jesus Christ. He told me *John 15:6: "If anyone does not remain in me, he is like a branch that is thrown away and withers; such branches are picked up, thrown into the fire and burned."* All this happened to me because God saw that this was the only way I would turn from my evil ways. *Jeremiah 18:11: "Now therefore say to the people of Judah and those living in Jerusalem, This is what the LORD says: Look! I am preparing a disaster for you and devising a plan against you. So turn from your evil ways, each one of you, and reform your ways and your actions."*

Now He is molding me according to His will. *(Jeremiah 18:1-6)* I am looking at sentences of life without parole or death. I have been serving God almost two years, and I rejoice daily. Serving Him is all to me. I have touched so many lives. I have helped people coming into jail who wanted to commit suicide give their lives to God. I have helped people in distress, anguish, turmoil, and without peace as they have come to me, and the Holy Spirit has worked through me. They rejoice and end up with peace in their lives. People ask me why I am so happy in a place like this. I just tell them I have Jesus in my life, and the next thing you know, they want what I have.

I lead three Bible studies every week in our pod, and I thank God for providing me with the knowledge and all that God has given me. I won't trade it for anything. To all those who have a case like mine and feel that God cannot use them, that's a lie of the devil. Prison is where you get built up. *(Colossians 2:6-7, 2 Timothy 2:19-21)*

Don't let anything stop you from serving the Lord. Like I said, it hasn't been fifteen years yet serving God, but I will tell you right now, I won't go back to serving the devil. *(Revelation 20:10, 15)* I'd rather see you all in heaven. *(Revelation 21:3-4)* With all sincerity, and truth, I close this letter with these words of encouragement. *"So, if the Son sets you free, you will be free indeed." (John 8:36)*

38. THE POWER OF PRAYER — Lloyd Henderson

On July 1, 2006, the Chaplain and a guest speaker enter pod 2200. She called out the afternoon worship. We all started to gather around to fulfill God's purpose, and while we were moving forward to exit the doors and walking down the hallway, before we came close to the elevators, we could hear and see two guys having an altercation. The devil was really playing his part. This is something that we never experienced before in worship time. As the two men were using vulgar and abusive language, their anger began to rise, like water in a boiling pot. I paused and I questioned myself, "Where is the love, peace, and kindness in their hearts?" They continued to savagely attack one another with words.

What a great way of showing maturity. They still have not realized that their fight was not about them. It was about the Lord, and why they were coming as we were waiting for the elevator. The power of the Lord moved us into a prayer circle We began saying the Lord's Prayer from *Matthew 6:9-13*. Still, we knew the devil was right there in the midst of it all, trying to tempt us and to destroy our spirit. We will never let the devil win as sure as my heart, my mind, and my gut were speaking. We all continued to go on to fellowship even though this situation had occurred.

This was an example for us all. *"When I was a child, I talked like a child, I thought like a child, I reasoned like a child. When I became a man, I put childish ways behind me."(1 Corinthians 13:11)* It could have turned out worse than it did, because, in this day and age, violence has begotten violence.

Stop and think. Life is too short! Think before you react to others and your surroundings so that you don't have to regret any foolish action or destructive behavior. Now you have to prove only one thing, the good inside your heart, for that is what the Lord Jesus Christ sees within you. You all have received the gifts of faith, hope, and love which come from God's armor.

39. A DOORWAY TO A NEW BEGINNING — Gabriel Salazer

On August 16, 2005, the door came crashing down, and one would think that my life would have come crashing down right along with the door! Do you want to know what my first silent thought was? It was, "FINALLY!" I was tired, and on top of being tired, I was doing badly; I can honestly say that's the worst I have ever been doing. There were seven law enforcement officers rushing through the doorway

I was picked up for a parole violation, but I knew it was a matter of time before new charges popped up. Sure enough, four days later I was sitting in C Module and my cell door burst open, I was told to go down to booking where I was told that eight new charges had popped up. They say that when you die, your life passes before your eyes. Now I cannot explain it, but as they read off the eight new charges, I saw my kids' faces, my mom, my girl friend, and the door. My life seemed to come crashing down: my life, the memories flashing right before my eyes, the good and the bad.

As I walked back to my pod, I just wanted to yell out. But I was so all alone and empty that no yell could've ever come out. *Psalms 7:15-16* says, *"He who digs a hole and scoops it out falls into the pit he has made. The trouble he causes recoils on himself; his violence comes down on his own head."* I went back to my cell, closed the door, and told my "celly" what had just happened down in booking. He is a man I have known for several years and is someone I consider a friend. You know, I was mad at him at first because he just laughed and told me to join the club! I thought — the club? I wanted to get down and club him on his head! Let's just say I didn't. He got up and turned off the light, and told me that I should pray, asking for forgiveness and guidance. He told me of how he had just signed off on a sixteen year deal and some of his family struggles. He told me how he had fallen on his face, cried out to God, and turned his life over to Him. He told me how he's never felt better and was full of joy, and even though he has to go back to prison, he feels good about his future.

As I lay there with his words just kind of ringing in my ears - pray - pray. I remembered that I used to pray, but I was ashamed to go to God in prayer. I was like a dog that wet the carpet again! Hours later, though, I finally prayed; but I only prayed for my kids, my mom, my family, my girl friend, and her family - but I forgot about me. I continued to pray like that for a few more weeks, maybe longer.

As time went on, I started attending worship services with some friends. I felt better. I attended a service where Chaplain John spoke, and I was moved. I felt as if he were speaking to me. I had to look around to see if anybody else was hearing this. The Holy Spirit filled that emptiness that I had. God was talking to me. So, I picked up a Bible, read it, went to church and Bible study regularly, and re-dedicated my life to Jesus. I began to pray for forgiveness, guidance, and a whole list of other things. But I was idle; I needed to do something else - not just for myself, either. I couldn't quite explain it.

One day at service, Chaplain McDonald was telling us about the *Maximum Saints* book project, and I stopped talking to my neighbor, because again I was moved. Something told me to listen because this was for me. I asked how I could participate in this project, she told me, and I wrote something. My writing made the book! Man, was I happy. I was full of joy, and then I knew what needed to be done.

I feel good when I write. Another thing is I have always wanted to help people, you know, keep them from making the same crazy mistakes I made. Now I am no chaplain, pastor, or scholar, but I hope you can hear me. I hope that you can benefit from something that I say or have said. I know I chose this craziness to be my life, but how many of you can hear me when I tell you that this kind of life is truly sad?

If you can't hear me, it's probably because you haven't lost enough, and I urge you to stop playing and living, this game! *Ecclesiastes 12:1* says: *"Remember your Creator in the days of your youth, before the days of trouble come and the years approach when you will say, 'I find no pleasure in them.'"* I am not just alive breathing, but alive in many different ways! My God has blessed me with this talent that makes me feel good about myself and the way I can express myself. More importantly, I bring glory to God by doing so! I ask you, has God spoken to you in some sort of way? Has He blessed you with a gift? Are you good at writing or maybe speaking? Can you draw, or are you a good teacher? If you said yes to any of these or to something that I didn't mention, then I say to you, do it, and thank God, and watch how good you'll feel. I feel alive! God has shown me His love and blessed me, and I have just begun. Now I would like to end this with the words my friend told me but with a little different meaning. "Join the club," not by doing time but by walking with Christ and praying for forgiveness and guidance. *Psalms 119:71 says, "It was good for me to be afflicted so that I might learn your decrees."* God bless you!

40. GOD COMFORTS US IN ALL OUR TROUBLES
— Erica Nieto

In the early part of my teenage years, I was a prisoner of myself. I was addicted to crack cocaine and in a relationship in which I was brutally beaten to the point of having a fractured jaw, shoe prints on my back, black eyes and bruises, not only on my body but on my soul. I took it all for love. I was only fourteen years old when all this started, and even when I got past the physical abuse from others, I abused myself mentally and physically with drugs and alcohol. From the age of fourteen until I was twenty-three, I was numb and hopeless.

I left home at fourteen and felt I had to do what I had to do to survive, not realizing that I was selling my soul. As a young girl on the streets, I kept on the move, going to many different places. I was trying to run away from myself all the time – running, running, always running. But everywhere I went, there I was. Nothing had changed. I've learned that, through all the severe abuse from others and myself and through the times I stared death in the face and lived to see another day, God was protecting me, letting me run myself tired.

I was tired of drowning in my own tears, tired from all the pain of feeling alone and neglected, not knowing that all along, I had had everything I needed to fill my heart. I had searched everywhere but in God and myself. All the hope and love I needed was there all long. All I had to do was ask God. *Matthew 7:7* says, *"Ask and it will be given to you, seek and you will find; knock and the door will be opened to you."* I see young girls and women who are empty and running from themselves, looking outside themselves for love and contentment, and I feel the desire to help them find what they're looking for. "I wish I had known then what I know now." I'd have saved myself a lot of tears, but then again, I wouldn't be the strong woman I am today, and most important of all, I wouldn't have the experiences to help others in need. God has definitely pulled me a long way from ten years ago. *Philippians 1:6* says, *"being confident of this, that he who began a good work in you will carry it on to completion until the day of Christ Jesus."*

There is no growth without change, no change without fear or loss, and no loss without pain. This is quoted from *The*

Purpose Driven Life, by Rick Warren: God says that everything we go through is to mold us. God uses our painful experiences to mold us the most. Our greatest ministry will come out of our greatest hurt! *2 Corinthians 1:4* teaches us that God comforts us in all our troubles so that we can comfort others. When others are troubled, we will be able to give them the same comfort God has given us. I read that if we really desire to be used by God, we must understand that the painful situations and most regretful experiences we've been through are not meant to be hidden, they are supposed to be used to help others. In order for God to use our painful experiences, we must share them.

Paul understood this, so he admitted *"We do not want you to be uninformed, brothers, about the hardships we suffered in the province of Asia. We were under great pressure, far beyond our ability to endure, so that we despaired even of life. Indeed, in our hearts we felt the sentence of death. But this happened that we might not rely on ourselves but on God, who raises the dead. He has delivered us from such a deadly peril, and he will deliver us."* (2 Corinthians 1:8-10a) *Ezekiel 17:1-14* describes how powerful God can be if we just listen to Him. God put life back into me and used my past as strong points for my new life.

41. I AM FREE — Salvador Aquilar

The day I got arrested, all I could think was, "When will I be free again? When will I get to go back to my life full of freedom?" I had been at a juvenile place for about five days when after court the judge said, "You're being direct filed." I wasn't quite sure what that was, but I knew it did not mean I was free to go.

I arrived at the ACDF that same day. It was night, and they placed me on suicide watch in a lonely room with just a mat to lie on. That night, the Holy Spirit came to me as I prayed for forgiveness and liberty. I asked God, "Why have you abandoned me?" He replied, "Your life is just a vain illusion. What was your liberty: drinking, being corrupt and wicked, and causing yourself and others problems? Are you free when you have to watch your back every time you go outside? Are you free when your mind is controlled by drugs? Ask yourself what freedom is."

All I could think about that night was, "What is freedom?" I knew I had to figure it out in order to be calm and fall asleep. I didn't sleep that night; neither did I figure out what God had said. Two days later I moved to the juvenile pod, it was a Thursday. I laid in my bed every time at lockdown and tried to figure out what was the real meaning of freedom. My mom came to visit me on Sunday. I could only see her through the screen, and I broke down in tears as I saw my mom's desperate face and my two sisters staring at me, thinking, "How could you do this to yourself?"

That night, as a stream of tears came flowing from my eyes, no one but God came to my life. He turned on the light in the dark tunnel. I followed and He set me free. Now I walk down the narrow path of the Lord. I know the Lord is kind and He forgives, what I thought was freedom, but He came and showed me the way to "true freedom," spiritual freedom. Now, I pray day and night this thing is over soon. The Lord will set me free because He forgives, and I will never go back to that dark tunnel. As I prayed once again for freedom and forgiveness, a sudden sense of freedom came to my mind, Jesus spoke to me: "Son, true freedom is spiritual freedom." There it was, the answer I was looking for. It all made sense; this means I am free in jail. Well, of course I'm not free to go out when I want or to do what I want, but I am spiritually free. Free because I have repented and Jesus Christ has forgiven my sins. May the Lord be with us all.

42. TO HIM WHO OVERCOMES — Charles Frederick

I have been to jail numerous times, and I'm sure, some of you can relate to that. I decided to start looking at my life and to try to figure out why I keep doing the things that land me right back in here. Who better to ask these questions of than my Creator, my Lord and Savior Jesus Christ? So I began reading my Bible and asking the Lord, "Lord, please show me in your Word what I need to do to live my life for you." As I started searching this out, one passage that really seemed to hit home was *Romans 12:1-2.*

Verse 1 says, *"Therefore, I urge you, brothers, in view of God's mercy, to offer your bodies as living sacrifices, holy and pleasing to God - this is your spiritual act of worship."* What the Lord seemed to be telling me was that if I wanted to serve Him, I needed to give Him my all. I could not hang on to the cares of this world, because if I hung on to them, I could not hang on to God. Verse 2 says, *"Do not conform any longer to the pattern of this world, but be transformed by the renewing of your mind. Then you will be able to test and approve what God's will is - his good, pleasing and perfect will."* Transformed? "Yes! This is what I am looking for, Lord. I want to be transformed for You. I do not want to continue to do these crazy, stupid, idiotic, foolish things that I have been doing for so long. I want to be transformed for you, God! I want to live for You!"

So, as I continued searching the Scriptures of God my King for understanding, I came across *I Corinthians 10:13.* *"No temptation has seized you except what is common to man. And God is faithful; he will not let you be tempted beyond what you can bear. But when you are tempted, he will also provide a way out so that you can stand up under it."* Okay God, here Your word tells me basically that temptations will arise but that you faithfully will provide a way for me to overcome these temptations. Then the Lord told me, " Charles, I became a man and walked the earth and I was tempted *(Hebrews 4:15-16).* What did I do when Satan tempted me in the wilderness? I used Scripture! Remember the Word, *"For our struggle is not against flesh and blood, but against the rulers, against the authorities, against the powers of this dark world and against the spiritual forces of evil in the heavenly realms."* (Ephesians 6:12) My word, is the sword of the Spirit. You must put my Word in your mind to fight these spiritual battles. Without my Word, you cannot overcome these worldly, selfish desires you battle daily." My eyes began to open. I finally started to understand what I needed to do to be transformed so that I could live my life for God. Remember that *Romans 12:2* says that we must be transformed by the renewing of our mind. To renew our minds, we must put God's Word into them so that we might be able to combat the wickedness we have been pumping into ourselves for numerous years.

Then I came across the passage in *Philippians 4:8* that says, *"Finally, brothers, whatsoever is true, whatever is noble, whatever is right, whatever is pure, whatever is lovely, whatever is admirable - if anything is excellent or praiseworthy - think about such things."* Listen to me, please, we cannot allow bad things to occupy our minds. The battle starts right here and right now in our minds. The devil tries to put bad thoughts in our minds, because if we're thinking about those things, we're not thinking about God. If you allow your mind to dwell for hours, reminiscing about your wicked past, then when you are released from here, that's what you're going to do. I am here to tell you today what God's Word says we need to do in order to change. We need to trust in God with all our heart (Proverb. 3:5-6) If you fully trust God, your life shows it because you start living how He tells you to live. If you are not being obedient to God, you are not trusting Him. His Word also says, *"I have hidden your Word in my heart that I might not sin against you." (Psalms 119:11)*

We must put God's Word in our heart so we can fight this spiritual battle. *Ephesians 6:17* clearly states that the sword of the Spirit is the Word of God. John gives a description of the Son of Man (Jesus) it says, *"Out of His mouth went a sharp two-edged sword." (Revelation 1:16a)* In other words, out of His mouth came the Word of God. This is what should be coming out of our mouths as well. *Hebrews 4:12* says, *"For the word of God is living and active. Sharper than any double-edged sword, it penetrates even to dividing soul and spirit, joints and marrow; it judges the thoughts and attitudes of the heart."*

The Word of God will help us fight the battle in our minds. We must grow spiritually. The Word of God is our spiritual food, and we must feed on it daily. I believe it is so much more important for us to feed our spirit than our flesh. As humans we can survive on just a little food each day. But, I am telling you, in this wicked, perverse, satanic society we are living in today, if you are not feeding your spirit a good, healthy diet of God's Word daily, the cares of this world will choke you. You cannot grow spiritually until you start being obedient to God!

Again, I want to emphasize the importance of memorizing God's Word. The Bible says to meditate on God's word day and night. (*Psalms 1:2*) When a bad thought enters your mind, stop it by quoting Scripture in your mind! If you allow wrong thinking in your mind, you are allowing Satan to muddle your thoughts. You must change that thinking with meditation on God's Word. By doing that, your mind will start being transformed so that you can prove to the rest of the world that God's Word is true and it does work in our lives.

Revelation 3:19-21 says, *"Those whom I love I rebuke and discipline. So be earnest, and repent. Here I am! I stand at the door and knock. If anyone hears my voice and opens the door, I will come in and eat with him, and he with me. To him who overcomes, I will give the right to sit with me on my throne, just as I overcame and sat down with my Father on His throne."* The Lord is knocking my friends, are you going to open the door? Are you going to live your way or God's way? Remember, to grow spiritually, we must start being obedient to what God says!

43. THE FEAR WITHIN US — Jonathan Willis

In life we experience many different types of fear. A fear can originate from practically anything. For instance, a lack of money, death, rejection, threats, change, guilt form things we have done, embarrassment, dependencies, the unknown, and failure. Just to name a few. You can see just by reading the list I have presented why it would be unreasonable for someone to say they are fear-free in life. That would be like someone telling you they are not human. We are all subject to fear. Since we are human and fear is a reality for us, we must learn how to conquer it. The only way to do so is to give all our fears over to God.

By nature we are sinful beings and unable to stand under the weight of the world without support. Listen to what Jesus said in *Matthew 7:24-25, "Therefore everyone who hears these words of mine and puts them into practice is like a wise man who built his house on the rock. The rain came down, the streams rose, and the winds blew and beat against that house; yet it did not fall, because it had its foundation on the rock."*

Jesus goes on to say in verses 26 and 27 what happens to a life built with no support. *"But everyone who hears these words of mine and does not put them into practice is like a foolish man who built his house on sand. The rain came down, the streams rose, and the winds blew and beat against that house, and it fell with a great crash."* When we let fear get the best of us our whole life is effected. Here is an example from my life.

In September of 2005, at the age of 23, I was living in Cincinnati, Ohio. I had just got fired from my job of 3 years at a pay scale of $27.50 per hour. It was nobody's fault but my own for getting fired. Being a young guy with a successful career and deep pockets, made my use of an abundance of drugs common place. I had been given many chances by my employer to share up. But my addiction was more powerful than any self driven will I could conjure up to quit. As a result, I called in late for the last time after staying up all night drinking and smoking cocaine. Needless to say, my job had had enough of my irresponsible behavior. I lost what I worked so hard for. What made matters worse, was that I couldn't find another job that would accept me without a driver's license and car, that was wiling to pay close to the same money. I had lost my license from D.U.I.'s and was riding to work with a friend who lived near by. None of the companies were willing to work with me. So my only other option was to settle for a job that would pay substantially less money.

During this low point in my life, I finally turned to God

for help. I decided to get involved with a good church that had a Bible study for recovering addicts. In the mean time I lost my apartment and moved in with my uncle. One day after job hunting I was going through some of my belongings and ran across a phone number. It was to a girl I hadn't talked to in about 2 years. I had met her 3 years prior and she lived out in Colorado. I decided to give her a call. While we were catching up on the past and discussing my present situation, she suggested that I move out to Colorado to live with her and her mother. She told me everything would be taken care of and she could drive me to work every day. I was proposed with an easier way out. Instead of facing my fear of being on the low end of the food chain in the eyes of others, and having patience with God's plan to restore me in His time, I jumped at the new opportunity.

Within weeks I was on a Greyhound to Colorado. All I did by relocating was bring my problems with me. I fell for the easier way out. The quick fix. My life from there on out was continually falling apart. As a result of my caving in to my fear of inferiority. Things ended up not working out between the female and I. I wasn't attending church anymore and I resorted back to getting high to escape the harsh reality. Thus rekindling the vicious cycle I tried to leave behind.

Now I am in jail facing life in prison. Just another example of what God will allow if we don't do our best to parallel to guidelines for living His so plainly spelled out for us in His word, the Bible. That initial compromise led to many more until resulting in my loss of freedom. I can't stress the point enough on how crucial it is to face fear head on instead of running and letting it snowball.

I am proud to share that I am now a born again member of the family of Christ Jesus our Savior. I have given my doubts, insecurities, and fears to God. God's shoulders are a heck of a lot stronger than ours. We need to share the burden of fear with Him to avoid cracking underneath it. You may ask how do I just give up my fears?

Step One: Confess to yourself and God what you are afraid of and recognize the reality of the fear.

Step Two: Realize that this life on earth is only temporary and the fact that heaven is waiting for us if we are saved. This will give you a proper perspective of your life and help you realize that your fears aren't really as big as they seem.

Step Three: Recognize the fact that conquering all your fear is not a possibility without God's help. Trust that God has power over our fears and that through Him anything is possible.

Psalm 46:1-2 says, *"God is our refuge and strength, an ever-present help in trouble. Therefore we will not fear, though the earth give way and the mountains fall into the hear of the sea."* I promise that your life will be forever changed for the better if you can learn to let God be your refuge and strength from fear. Here are some words of encouragement from *2 Timothy 1:7, "For God did not give us a spirit of timidity, but a spirit of power, of love and of self-discipline."* In closing, I just want to let you know that the best things in life are free. So is freedom from fear.

44. AN ARTISTIC ENVELOPE FOR VETERANS AT WAR ACTIVITY — Carlos Tanguma

I would like to introduce you to "Artistic Envelopes Project for Veterans at War Activity," an art club in which inmates at Adams County Detention Facility in Brighton, Colorado, are participating. This club, also known as "Inmates to Angels," uses jailhouse art as a means for decorating envelopes. The soldiers and families of people at war receive hope, joy, and comfort when they receive these original hand-drawn and skillfully colored envelopes with which they can mail their letters. Our prayers go out to anyone who receives these envelopes. I am a Christian inspired by God's healing grace to do something helpful and inspirational for anyone serving in or affected by this most serious war. I pray with you for peace. Sincere heartfelt prayers, acts of kindness, soul searching, and self-sacrifice are some of what our soldiers, family and friends of military personnel are feeling and living.

Some inmates also go through these same feelings and dilemmas while seeking change and understanding. Chaplain has a vision of spiritual revival of jailhouse ministries and healing for inmates. I agree with that vision. In fact that call helped inspire this art club. Revival will bring healing. Revival is a gift of forgiveness, love, change of heart and turning away from contrary lifestyles and activities that hurt society, our families, ourselves, and lead to more severe punishments and laws.

Friends, please contribute to this art club. Use it to turn on your heart light. Share, heal, and forgive yourself and others through your art. Let the good that God created in you bring comfort and joy to our loved ones and friends at war. Get a blank envelope, search your heart, and decorate the front of it with compassion to help others. I promise you, you won't regret it! Draw a masterpiece as a comfort for people at war. It's worth it, sisters and brothers. It's worth your effort to be on the side of life of peace, joy, love, and sanctification received from our Creator for selfless giving.

Everyone has been down a bumpy road and dragged others with them. Now let God use you and your artistic gifts for His glory. Step out of your comfort zone! Prove yourself worthy, says the Lord…when the hours of work are done; the soul searching, the caring and compassion …comes the payoff. In Heaven, you've laid up your treasures. As Jesus said, "Freely, you have received! Freely give!" God has given me the desire to spread this artistic ministry, and I would like to share how God brought healing in some participants.

When I speak to someone about participating in this activity, I tell them, "Only do it if your heart tells you to do it." I have been personally moved when people who I knew were on an emotional roller coaster "donated" beautifully decorated envelopes. Some participants have not had any contact or support from family or friends. Some have the added weight of a language barrier. Some do not participate, but the chances keep opening up.

One participant's art work was mostly of a biblical theme. Over the months, I had been cut short or given the "look" when I tried to speak to him about God. He was mad at God and hurt that absolutely no one had sent a letter or any money. His mom had recently passed away. Since he was a very busy artist with considerable talent, and I was raised with a career Chicano artist, I kept getting opportunities to talk with him about art, family, and of course, God. Finally, I showed him some of my stick figure art drawings that I made to get the club going. I asked him if he would donate a work. Well, this man turned out to be a big participant and always drew with a gospel theme. His art work seemed to be helping him. I noticed that he became more at peace with himself and was opening up to the forgiveness and healing aspect of dealing with family that had hurt him and life itself.

I believe there is a need to minister to Latinos who speak little English and are doing time in jail. Many times their families aren't even in this country. A buddy of mine had lost everything. All his clothes, electronics, and money reserves were taken by a co-worker after he was arrested. I am happy to see him studying English. What draws me to him is that he acts like a child of God even in the midst of much peer pressure to the contrary. His wife, child and family are in Tabasco, Mexico. When I spoke to this man about the art club, I told him that 10,000 Mexicans who aren't even US citizens are at war in Iraq and Afghanistan. I said, "So, please search your heart to see if you'd like to contribute."

Four days later, he contributed two envelopes: one with the Virgin of Guadalupe and the other with a hand holding a cross. This art work is all hand drawn and gives the participants time to meditate about God while doing something for someone else.

Another inmate works all day, has a serious illness, and is an army veteran. He has spent hours turning himself into an artist, and he has donated some incredible flower art, motivated by the knowledge that someone will choose his work to communicate a letter to a loved one. It is to God's glory that this person attains the strength and motivation to participate. It takes me about three hours to do one envelope. The peace and focus I experienced in the last eleven months while I've been studying God's Word while creating art is worship in itself. *"The king will reply, 'I tell you the truth, whatever you did for one of the least of these brothers of mine, you did for me.'" (Matthew 25:40)*

45. MAKE NO LITTLE PLANS, MAKE BIG PLANS
 — Chaplain McDonald

After World War I, The Chicago Temple, the First United Methodist Church in downtown Chicago, reached a critical point. People were moving out of the downtown area, and the church's membership was shrinking. Some members thought that they should sell the church building and move to the suburbs, but this church had visionary leaders who inspired the congregation to envision a bigger sanctuary that would seat one thousand people and a twenty-six-story high building with beautiful architecture that would prepare the church for the future.

The architect, Daniel Burnham, made a famous speech: "Make no little plans....make big plans; aim high in hope and work....Let your church be order and your beacon beauty....think big." His vision for the church project was approved, and the new church building was dedicated on Easter morning in 1952. Each year, thousands of people make a pilgrimage to visit Chicago Temple. I had the privilege of visiting this church and was inspired by the beautiful architecture of the sanctuary, and the building.

This church is growing in membership, and also in ministry opportunities, because over the period of time since the new church was built, big apartment complexes have been built, and the population grew. Also, this church developed mission programs to feed the poor and homeless, and developed art ministry. All of this was possible because they made big plans.

This story teaches us a great spiritual lesson. We have to be visionaries if we want to serve God. We need to make big plans to serve God's kingdom. Unless we plan it, we are not going to see the result. God made big plans to save people from sin and eternal hell through Jesus. God made big plans to save us through Jesus. *"God so loved the world that He gave His one and only Son, that whoever believes in Him shall not perish but have eternal life." (John 3:16)* Jesus also told us to make big plans to save people. He said, *"Therefore go and make disciples of all nations...baptize them...teaching them to obey everything I have commanded you." (Matthew 28:19-20a)* Jesus believes that we have great potential and can make a difference in the world. He said, *"I tell you the truth, anyone who has faith in me will do what I have been doing. He will do even greater things than these, because I am going to the Father." (John 14:12)*

Jesus has the power to help us. He pulls us out of a pit if we ask Him for help. Jesus has faith in us, even when we make mistakes. When we ask Jesus for forgiveness, He forgives us. He brings healing when we are wounded and hurting. He carries us when we don't have the strength to walk. He gives us directions as to how we can serve Him by serving others by the power of the Holy Spirit. He gives us the power to resist the devil.

The sad thing is that many Christians make little plans, even though we say that we want to serve the Lord. Many of us are making plans that are too little and are thinking about only our own comfort. We need to stretch our minds in accordance with God's will. Jesus' plan should come first before anything else. If your plan for the future is only taking care of yourself and your family and is focused only on your financial security, you have made little plans in accordance only with your own will.

I want to give you a few suggestions: For those of you who have not accepted Jesus as your personal Savior, make big plans for your eternity to be with the Lord by giving your life to

Christ. You will make the best investment for your soul when you recognize that God can forgive you and save you. For those of you who are Christians but making only little plans, start asking God to give you visions and dreams of how you can make plans to serve God to the maximum.

Remember, God's big plans always move us beyond our comfort zones. God's big plans always include that we hear, see, understand and feel the pain and suffering of others, and do something about it. Moses had a little plan when God called him. Moses thought about his own comfort and tried to give God excuses why he wouldn't be the right person to deliver the Israelites. When Moses obeyed God's plan, he was able to free the Israelites from slavery. I believe God has big plans for all of us because Jesus can do much more than we can think or imagine. We all have goodness in us because we are created in the image of God. God's creativity and many other holy characteristics are part of our nature. If you see only bad in yourself and others, you have not seen all of what God has created. God is calling us to exercise that goodness by asking us to love God and love our neighbors. Until we can exercise those characteristics and practice our goodness by loving God and loving our neighbors, we cannot be happy or feel fulfilled. Deepest joy and fulfillment can come only when we love God and our neighbors.

What about us? Do we have faith in us as much as Jesus has faith in us? Do we believe that we can make a difference in this world? Don't tell me that you don't have any special gifts. When we look into what we have, we can see that we have received many gifts. The most important gift each one of us has been given is our very life. Unfortunately, many people do not take care of God's gift of life. They misuse their bodies and do destructive things to themselves and others. Yet, our creativity and our compassion are gifts from God. Our desires to be good and to do good, are God given characteristics and are gifts. Our faith is a gift from God to be shared with others, and this takes planning and commitment. Your encouraging words of faith can be life saving gifts to those who do not know Christ and to those who want to grow in Christ.

Make big plans, and ask God to give you directions for reaching your goal. Then be ready because the devil will try to convince you that working for God is too difficult for you or that you don't have the gifts to do it. The devil will try to convince you that you are not good enough to do God's work. Don't listen to the devil's lies. If you do, you will end up making little plans and grieving the Lord.

To make big plans, start with what you have. Ask God how you can serve Him to the maximum with what you have. One way of examining your heart to see whether you have a big plan or a little plan, is to see if you have the passion to save the lost. If you don't feel the burden for the lost, you are making little plans. Another way of examining your heart is to see if your plan is easily achievable. If it is, then probably your plan is too little. Every big plan for the kingdom of God stretches our imagination and goes beyond our limited thinking. Sometimes it looks impossible to reach the goal. Also, if you make plans without being willing to pay the price, you are actually making little plans. Jesus said we cannot be His disciples unless we deny ourselves, pick up our cross and follow him. The price you have to pay is this: You have to discard your own plans and make Jesus' plan your first priority.

Sometimes, even when we think we have made big plans to serve God, we still come up short. I am learning that through the book project, *Maximum Saints*. By the end of February 2006, with the help of many churches and friends, I was able to raise enough funds to order 1,500 copies of *Maximum Saints* Since ACDF had about 1,300 inmates, I knew 1,500 copies would be enough. God spoke to my heart that my vision was too small. So, I ordered 10,000 copies of the book for ACDF and for other jails and prisons in Colorado. God provided all the funds.

Make big plans to serve God. That's the only way you can find happiness in this life. Even though you might be going through the fires of testing, if you make big plans to help others, you will come out with joy. If you don't make big plans, you will find that there is a big, empty hole in your heart that nothing can fill. This is one way the Holy Spirit communicates with us. When you have a restless heart, you need to learn to listen to the heart of God to make big plans.

If you know that something is missing in your life even after you have become a Christian, it's about time that you think about making big plans to serve God. If you don't make big plans, the price you will be paying will be great. It might be that you live in misery and depression because you are only looking into your own pain, and as much as you dwell in your own pain and suffering, your wounds will grow, and it will overwhelm you. When you start looking into others' pain and start helping them, your wounds will heal.

For those of you who are anxious to leave this facility to go home, I want you to examine your heart to see what you are planning to do when you get out. If you are making little plans to serve yourself by getting drunk and using drugs, the results are always the same. You will end up living in turmoil, and there is a chance that you will be coming back to the facility for more "training."

If you make big plans to serve God and are committed to follow your plans no matter what happens, it will happen to you. If you make big plans, are you willing to pay the price to follow your calling and use your gifts to the maximum, no matter where you are? The price you have to pay is to put God's kingdom first, above everything else, no matter what happens. It's time that you realize that little plans cannot help build God's kingdom but bring only misery and discontent.

You will get hurt when you make little plans to serve only yourself. Whatever the price you pay to obey the Lord will be worth it because the Holy Spirit will be blessing you with joy and peace. You can also see your incarceration as God's call to mission work to save people from going to hell. Be persistent. Big plans have to be accompanied by preparation. Work toward your goal every day, moment by moment. They have to be carefully planned and need our total commitment and dedication to follow the Holy Spirit's leading. Let me leave you with a couple of questions: How many people are you planning to lead to the Lord in your lifetime? If you come up with a number, how are you planning to achieve that goal? May God bless you in your making of big plans to serve the Lord and others.

Part Three:
Poems

Drawing "A Praying Saint" by Charles Polk

46. RICH — Juan Velasquez

Poor? No, of course not! In fact, I have much worth
because my riches are stored in heaven not here on earth.
Tired? Yes! So tired sometimes that I just can't cope.
But when I read *Hebrews 11:36-40*, my cup is over-filled with
hope. Lonely? More than you can imagine, almost everyday…
But I know He walks with me and guides me along the way.
Burdens? Hon, I have many, oftentimes too many to ignore.
So, I lean a little harder and trust Him even more.
Worthy? Oh no, not ever! But the wonder of it is that
He loves me in spite of myself and says I'm His.
And so I'm rich! Rich beyond words.
More rich than I've ever known…
Because my King died for me and made me
co-heir to His throne.

47. DIRECTIONS TO OUR FATHER'S HOUSE
 — Latonda Morgan Pina

Make a right onto Believeth Boulevard.
Keep straight and go to the Bridge of Faith
Which is over troubled water. When you get off the bridge,
Make a right turn and keep straight
You are on the King's Highway - heaven bound.
Keep going for three miles, one for the Father, one for the Son,
And one for the Holy Spirit. Then exit off to Grace Boulevard,
From there make a right turn on Gospel Lane.
Keep straight and make another right onto Prayer Road.
As you go your way, yield not to the traffic on Temptation
Avenue. Avoid also Sin Street for it is a dead end.
Pass by Envy Drive and Hate Avenue, along with Hypocrisy
Street, Gossiping Lane, and Backbiting Boulevard. However,
you have to go down Long-suffering Lane and Persecution
Boulevard, entering onto Trials and Tribulations Avenue, but
that's all right because Victory Street is straight ahead.

48. WHY DO YOU STILL LOVE ME? — Timothy Tice

I pray for Your guidance to open my eyes to heal my blindness.
You know my heart. You're in my soul.
I find it so hard at times to do what I'm told
I love my family, the ones you have blessed me with
I'll always love them even though they've quit
I once held them safely in my arms.
Now I give them to You I pray for their salvation is all I can
do…

So I am on my knees wondering since everybody else is gone
Why Lord do you still love me? I've given you all my needs
I came to you with a broken heart, living a life of sin
You came to me with love and didn't care where I had been.
I came to you with nothing not wanting to love.
You came to me with love and gave me respect among men.

All my dreams, wishes and needs…Could never compare with
the greatness you had for me…I give you my all
And pray God never again to ever let me fall…
Take my hand, my Lord and Savior.
Take me Jesus to the Promise Land

When the world can be so cruel and the ones you love don't
seem to care…Go to your knees and pray.
The love of Jesus Christ will always be there…
Why is unity so important?
I know how you feel, terrible long with dark emptiness
and yet Christ is the one in love with you

So what are we to do? Subject as we are to human weakness
We are baptized by one Spirit into one body.
Just as you were called to give hope when you were called
One Lord, one faith, one baptism
One God and father of all who is over all
and through all and in all.

Part Four:
Prayers

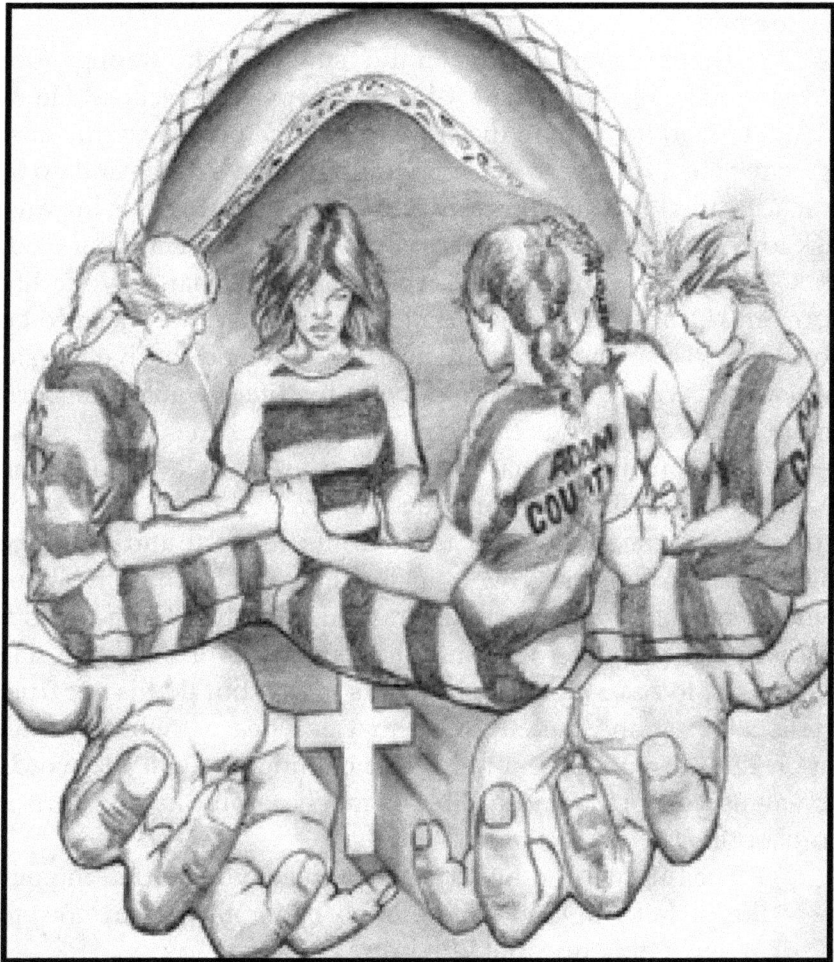

Drawing "Praying Saints" by Charles Polk

49. A NEW LIFE PRAYER — Angela Vasquez

Jesus said, *"In reply Jesus declared, 'I tell you the truth, no one can see the kingdom of God unless he is born again.'"* *(John 3:3)* God sent Jesus into the earth so that we could believe in Him and have eternal life. *(John 3:16)* This is what we call "becoming a Christian."

All of us on earth commit sins and do wrong. (see *Romans 3:23-26*) Only Jesus Christ was perfect because He is God. He died for you on the cross to pay the price for your sins. He gave His life for you, so you would not have to die and go to a place called hell. If you pray and ask Jesus into your life and ask for your sins to be forgiven, you will become a child of God. Take a minute and pray this prayer, it will change your life forever. "Dear God, I realize that I am a sinner and I need to be forgiven. Please come into my heart and life and forgive my sin and all the wrong things I've done in my life. I want to be born again and become your child. In Jesus' name. Amen!"

If you prayed that prayer, you are now a child of the Almighty God! You are forgiven and washed clean from all of your sins. I encourage you to continue to pray and read the Bible, so that you can grow as a Christian and learn more about what it means to be His child. Prayer is simply talking to God. Sometimes, we may feel intimidated by it or feel that He expects us to have all the right words to say, but that is not true. He is a loving and merciful God that will hear us when we call upon Him. If you have a hard time coming up with the words to say as you pray, find a Bible verse that you like and turn it into a prayer.

The following prayers are to help get you started in your new life of faith in God. There is no better time than now to begin a new habit, one that will bring peace and joy.

(1) Repentance:
"Dear Lord Jesus, I ask you humbly to forgive my sins. I ask that you would cleanse my mind, my heart and my spirit. I repent of the sins that I'm aware of and those that I am not. Cast

me not away from your presence and renew a right spirit within me. Please take away anything that would separate me from your love. Lord, I take responsibility for my actions, but I also accept your forgiveness. Help me to see myself as you see me, that I could also forgive myself. Thank you, Jesus, Amen." (*Psalms 51:10-11, 2 Peter 3:8-9*)

(2) <u>Faith (Believing and Trusting God)</u>:
"Dear God, I thank you that we can do nothing to earn your grace, it is a gift. I pray that you would help me now in this time of struggle to see that you are with me. I trust that you have a plan and a purpose for my life. Please help me to have more faith that you are working out everything in my life for the better. I give all control to you and ask that you would strengthen me and others around me. In Jesus' name I pray. Amen." (*Hebrews 11:1, 6, Matthew 7:7-8*)

(3) <u>Addictions and Ungodly Life Patterns</u>:
"Father God, please help me to let go of the things that are destructive. I bind the spirit of addiction in Jesus' name. I pray you would deliver me from alcohol, drugs, lust and every other ungodly life pattern that I have been living in. I pray that you would remove every craving and memory that would draw me back into temptation. Please give me the mind of Christ even as I sleep that my mind would not be a playground for Satan. I pray that you would fill the void in my life that I have tried to fill with so many other things. I pray for others in my life that have the same addictions that you would also set them free. In Jesus name I pray. Amen." (*Proverbs 21:31, John 8:36, 2 Timothy 4:18, Hebrews 4:15-16, 12:1-3, 1 John 2:15-17*)

(4) <u>Family and Friends</u>:
"Dear Lord, thank you for the people you have placed in my life. Forgive me for any pain I have caused them, and I also forgive and release them for any pain they have caused me. Please protect them as only you can. And I ask that you would

bring us back together quickly. Help me to be a better example and that they could see you in my life. I pray in the name of Jesus. Amen." (*Psalms 28:8-9, 9:9-10*)

(5) Children:

"Father God, we are your children. Show us how to be more like you as a parent. I pray for my children. I am sorry for letting them down. I ask that you would pour out your blessings in their lives and fulfill the plans that you have for them. I commit to do everything I can to be a better parent and show my children your love. Help fill the void in their lives while I'm away, and protect them. In Jesus' name I pray. Amen." (*Proverbs 22:6, Isaiah 54:13*)

(6) Court Hearings:

"Lord, I ask for your peace as I go before the judge. I ask that your will would be done in my life. I pray that you would give me favor and mercy. I pray against fear and doubt, for you have not given us a spirit of fear, but of power, love and sound mind. Help me to believe in you and to know that, no matter what happens, you are in control. Thank you for your mercy and grace. Help me to be kinder and more merciful to others and to treat others how I would want to be treated. In Jesus' name." Amen. (*Psalms 35:22-24, Romans 8:31-35*)

(7) Wisdom and Understanding:

"Dear Lord Jesus, I ask for wisdom, not as the world knows it, but heavenly wisdom. Help me to see things as you see them. Teach me to see sin as you do. I pray that you would give me more desire to read the Bible and help me understand as I read. Give me direction and goals for my life, so I can follow the plan you have set for me. Change the way I think, and help me put others before myself. Amen." (*Proverbs 3:13-15, 9:10, 10:31, 16:20, James 1:5*)

(8) Hope and Restoration:
"Jesus, the Bible says that Satan has come to steal, kill and destroy, but you have come to give us life more abundantly. I pray that you would restore all that Satan has destroyed in my life and in the lives of those I love. Please give me hope for my future and help me to remember the plans that Satan has for me when he tries to tempt and trick me. Give me the strength to fight back. Amen." *(Romans 5:5, Psalms 62:5-8, Isaiah 40:31, John 10:10)*

(9) Comfort of the Holy Spirit:
"I thank you, God, that you sent the Holy Spirit to bring us comfort in time of need. Please fill me with the Holy Spirit and those in my life that also need His touch. Please lead and guide me by the Spirit, and help me to never turn away from you. I pray that as you comfort me, I can in turn, comfort others around me. In Jesus' name I pray. Amen." *(Luke 11:9-13, John 14:16-17, Acts 1:8, 2:1-4, 2:38-39)*

(10) Forgiveness:
"Lord, I lay down all my unforgiveness towards others. I bless and release them into your hands. I realize that this is a choice and not an emotion. Help me to let go of bitterness, anger, hatred and revenge. Please fill my heart with love, just as you have loved me when I was in need of forgiveness. Thank you for your mercy. Teach me to be merciful to others. In Jesus' name. Amen." *(Matthew 6:12, Mark 11:25, Luke 6:35, 37, Ephesians 4:31-32, Colossians 3:13)*

(11) Thanksgiving:
"Most of all, God, I want to thank you for everything that you've done for me and will continue to do. Even in hard times, I know you are with me and you only want the very best for me. Help me to praise you and love you at all times, through the good and bad. I love you, Jesus. Amen."

50. A SEVEN WEEK PRAYER PROJECT: "A REVIVAL AND HEALING OF OUR SOULS" – Chaplain McDonald

"If my people, who are called by my name, will humble themselves and pray and seek my face and turn from their wicked ways, then will I hear from heaven and will forgive their sin and will heal their land. Now my eyes will be open and my ears attentive to the prayers offered in this place." (2 Chronicles 7:14-15)

When we become Christians, our spirits are born and we are like spiritual babies. If we want to grow, we need to take care of our spiritual matters and nurture ourselves. To grow in faith and have a deeper relationship with Jesus, I believe spiritual discipline is a must. Jesus said, "Follow me." Following Jesus is not easy because many Christians have not grown, and don't even know how to crawl. To learn to crawl: to eventually walk and follow Jesus takes discipline, persistence, determination, and commitment to live a holy life. Our spiritual growth is dependent on how we plan and follow through on those plans. One approach to spiritual growth I have found helpful, is to have a time of fasting and prayer.

I invite you to join a seven week prayer and fasting, to pray for a revival, and healing of our souls. You can join this prayer anytime and anywhere; as a group or as an individual. I am asking you to participate in it by following four spiritual practices.

1. Meditation

First, read one Gospel (Matthew, Mark, Luke or John) a day or one chapter of the Gospel a day to get to know Jesus. Also, read Romans, Isaiah, Jeremiah or whatever God will lead you to read. Try to read the Bible for 30 minutes or more every day for the next seven weeks. God speaks to us through Scriptures many times. It's a great way to listen to God's voice. When you need to hear God's voice, the Holy Spirit will remind you of the Scriptures. So, keep reading and praying so the Holy Spirit will give you wisdom to understand it. Also, try to read books that will help you grow in faith. Avoid any ungodly T.V. programs which will fill your heart with sinful desires.

2. Prayer

Here are seven prayer suggestions: You can also write your own. You can pray as you walk around the house or anywhere seven times and try to spend a half of the time talking to God in prayer and also a half of the time try to listen by inviting Jesus to talk you. "Lord Jesus, I am listening. Please speak to me. If there is any sin I need to repent or is there anything you would like to share with me, please help me to understand your heart."

(1) Pray for repentance: "Lord Jesus, please forgive my sins and help me to repent if there is sin I haven't repented. God bless me and this nation with the spirit of repentance so we can be saved and understand our spiritual condition. Help us to understand others' pain when we hurt them. Start it with me first Lord. Help me live a godly life that will please you. Forgive me all my sins and if there is any sin that I need to repent, please help me repent."

(2) Pray for wisdom to understand the Bible: "Holy Spirit, help me to have wisdom, knowledge, understanding, and revelation so I can understand the Word of God and live accordingly. Fill me with spiritual wisdom that I can live a holy life."

(3) Pray to experience Holy Spirit: "God, I give all my worries and fear to your powerful hands. Fill my heart with the Holy Spirit's peace and joy. Help me to develop a relationship with Jesus and the Holy Spirit so I can understand that you are real."

(4) Pray to understand the Holy Spirit's voice: "Holy Spirit, speak to me clearly. Guide and direct me and help me to have a willing heart so I can follow you and obey you."

(5) Pray to understand God's plans for you: "God, help me to

understand your plans, visions, and dreams for me so I can follow your plans instead of making my own plans and fall into sin."

(6) <u>Pray for a new heart</u>: "God, I ask for a new heart so I can follow you instead of following the worldly sinful desires. Please deliver me from all the cravings of sin and desires which will make me fall into temptation and sin. Wash me with the blood of Jesus and empower me to do what you want me to do."

(7) <u>Pray to raise the workers</u>: "God forgive me and others who sinned against you. Raise godly workers for your kingdom inside and outside prison walls. I pray for all the incarcerated and their families, especially children for God's leading in their lives. Please help me break the cycle of incarceration with your power and love. Provide godly Christian mentors for the children of the incarcerated."

You can also add personal prayer for 30 days and pray until God answers your prayers.

I would like to emphasize listening prayer in silence here because many do not hear God's voice because they talk too much to God and do not know how to wait before God. Every day practice listening prayer for 30 minutes in silence. Try to pray fifty per cent of your prayer time in talking and fifty per cent of your time to clear your mind. When you try to listen, ask God a question, and then clear your mind and listen in silence. Then, when you hear a voice in your mind, examine the voices through the Scriptures to see, if you heard Him or not. Remember, our mind is a spiritual battle field and you need to read the Bible to discern what is God's voice, and what is the devil's voice. Any thoughts which are destructive,

4. Fast

If you can, fast one meal a week for Saturday dinner for the next seven weeks. For those of you who want to fast but have medical problems when you miss a meal, I suggest that you not skip the meal, but please join the prayer anyway. Drink as much water or other liquids as you can while fasting, so you don't get dehydrated. Refrain from too much exercise while fasting, or you will feel drained. Try to be involved in only holy conversations, which can help you and others to grow in faith.

Understand that the devil might try to attack you to stop your fasting. All Christians are in a spiritual war, regardless. If you get into a situation where you become very agitated, stop reacting, and think about what is happening to you. Don't get into any arguments, but walk away from the situation before you lose your temper. The devil loves to see you lose your temper and do things that you will regret later. Don't give your heart and body to destruction, but glorify God. (*Romans 12:1-2*)

5. Help others who are hurting

I encourage you to look around and see if there are others who need your kind, encouraging words. Listen to the voice of the Holy Spirit and obey Him. This is a beginning of your great journey of growing spiritually if you obey. Many suffer from the spirit of judging others and critical spirit. Try to ask God to help you to see good in others and bless those who misunderstand you. Every time you start looking at others with judgmental attitudes, start praying for that person and bless them. If you are in a solitary, you just have to pray for those who have hurt you and who need your forgiveness. Pray for others and bless those who need your forgiveness. Share Christ whenever you can with your testimony how God has helped you and invite people to accept Christ to be saved.

Jesus said, *"The harvest is plentiful but the workers are few."* (*Matthew 9:37*) All Christians are called to be the harvesters. Let's pray so our faith comes alive and we can all overcome sinful desires and passion. When that happens, God can help us build up the kingdom of God and destroy the work of Satan.

For those who do not have a relationship with Jesus, open your heart to accept him. Jesus died on the cross for you so you can be forgiven.

Jesus said, *"For God so loved the world that he gave his one and only Son, that whoever believes in him shall not perish but have eternal life."(John 3:16)* If you want to invite Jesus, here is the prayer: "Lord Jesus, I invite you in to my heart and please forgive all my sins. Bless me with a new heart filled with desires to get to know you. Help me understand the Word of God so I can obey you. Help me to be filled with the Holy Spirit and help me to understand your plans, visions, and dreams for my life. Deliver me from any addictive sinful thoughts and behaviors. Help me to live a holy life. I made a decision to follow you and serve you. I pray this in Jesus name. Amen."

After this prayer, read the Bible, pray, forgive yourself, forgive others, attend church and share with others what God has done for you. Peter said, *"Repent and be baptized, everyone of you, in the name of Jesus Christ for the forgiveness of sins. And you will receive the Holy Spirit."(Acts 2:38)*

Part Five:
An Invitation

1. AN INVITATION TO ACCEPT CHRIST: HE IS TRULY THERE FOR US — Edmundo Jimenez

I was misled by others and fell into the devil's trap. But now with the help of Jesus and the Word of the Lord, I have given my soul to Him and asked for forgiveness of all of my sins. I truly believe that God never left me, and that He has forgiven me for what I have done. Now I know that He is with me all day, every day, because I have allowed Him into my heart. I am glad that I am in this place now because I have accepted Him into my heart and as my savior. He promised that all you have to do is close your eyes and say a prayer. The way I accepted Him was written in a book, *Maximum Saints Never Hide In The Dark,* "An Invitation Prayer."

This is what the book says, "Bow down, let the One who created the world lift your burdens and cleanse your soul. Let Jesus' love, hope, and joy fill you to the maximum. Jesus can help you deal with pain when no one else can. He can give you peace when no one else can. Here is a prayer that you can pray if you would like to invite Christ into your heart so you can be saved, and experience the peace of Christ in your heart."

Prayer: "Dear Jesus, I am prepared to invite you into my heart, mind, body and soul. I come before you, offering myself as a living sacrifice, confessing my sins and weaknesses. Father, I put all my trust in you, and I want you to have total control over my life. I am sorry, Lord, for the things I did that grieve you and others. Please forgive me for all of my sins. I ask that distractions around me be put on hold so that I will be able to receive you in my life today. Please send Your Holy Spirit into my heart, and give me the power to live a new life in Christ. Thank you, Lord, for your love, and I give my life to you in the name of Jesus. Amen."

"If you confess with your mouth, 'Jesus is Lord,' and believe in your heart that God raised Him from the dead you will be saved." (Romans 10:9) "If we confess our sins, he is faithful and just and will forgive us our sins and purify us from all unrighteousness." (1 John 1:9) "Jesus answered, 'I am the way and the

truth and the life. No one comes to the Father except through me." (John 14:6)

2. An Invitation for The Transformation Project Prison Ministry (TPPM):

Books and DVDs produced by TPPM are distributed in many jails, prisons and homeless shelters nationwide free of charge made possible by grants and donations. America has 2.3 million people incarcerated, the largest prison population in the world, and there is a great shortage of inspirational books in many jails and prisons.

"One Million Dream Project"

In 2010, TPPM board decided to expand the ministry goal, and started the "One Million Dream Project."TPPM decided to raise enough funds to distribute one million copies of each book that TPPM has produced for prisoners and homeless people. I ask you to pray for this project so God can help TPPM to reach out to those who cannot speak for themselves and are in need of spiritual guidance.

TPPM is a 501(c)(3) nonprofit organization, so your donation is 100% tax deductible. If you would like to be a partner in this very important mission of bringing transformation through the message of Christ in prisons and homeless shelters, or want to know more about this project, please visit: www.maximumsaints.org. You can donate on line or you can write a check addressed to:

Transformation Project Prison Ministry
5209 Montview Boulevard
Denver, CO 80207

Website: www.maximumsaints.org
Facebook: http://tinyurl.com/yhhcp5g

3. How to Purchase *Maximum Saints* Books:

This is for individuals who would like to purchase or send a copy to their incarcerated family. TPPM receives lots of requests for individual distribution but we only distribute them through chaplains. All the proceeds from *Maximum Saints* will go to TPPM to distribute more free books and DVDs to prisons and homeless shelters.

To find out more about purchasing *Maximum Saints* books, check our website: www.maximumsaints.com. The following *Maximum Saints* Books are available:

Book One: *Maximum Saints Never Hide in the Dark*
Book Two: *Maximum Saints Make No Little Plans*
Book Three: *Maximum Saints Dream*
Book Four: *Maximum Saints Forgive*
Book Five: *Maximum Saints All Things Are Possible*

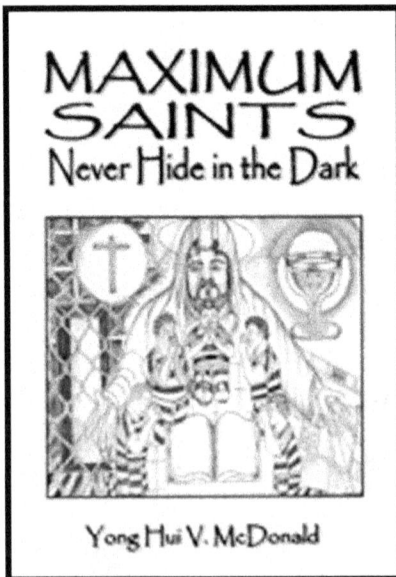

MAXIMUM
SAINTS
Never Hide in the Dark

Yong Hui V. McDonald

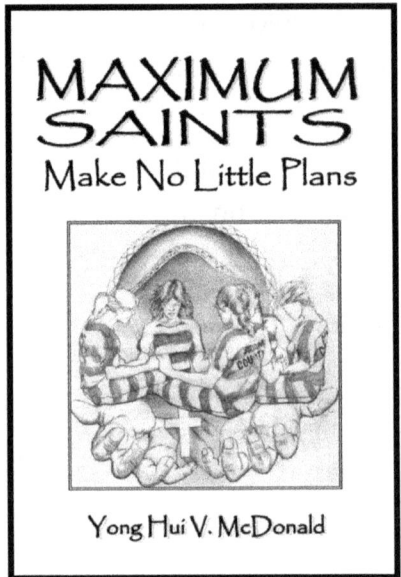

MAXIMUM
SAINTS
Make No Little Plans

Yong Hui V. McDonald

MAXIMUM
SAINTS
DREAM

Yong Hui V. McDonald

MAXIMUM
SAINTS
FORGIVE

Yong Hui V. McDonald

MAXIMUM
SAINTS
All Things Are Possible

Yong Hui V. McDonald

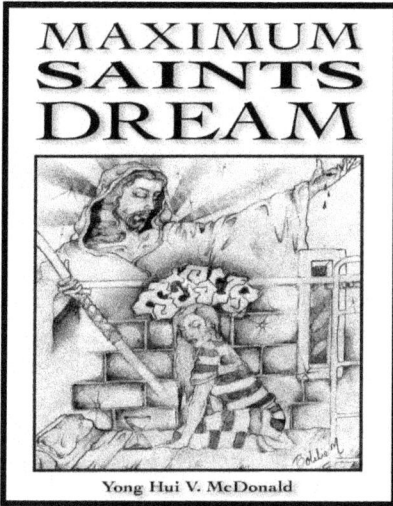

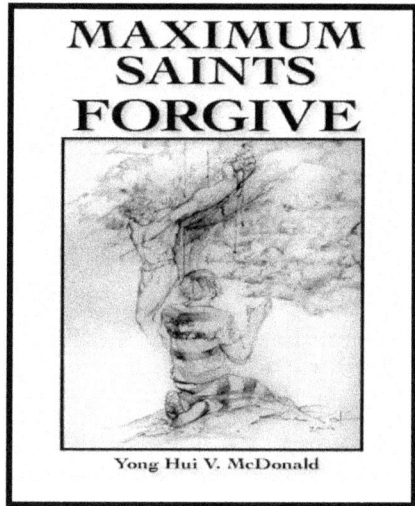

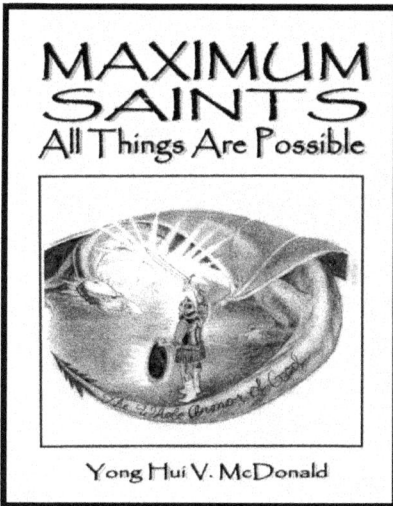

ABOUT THE AUTHOR

Yong Hui V. McDonald, also known as Vescinda McDonald, is a chaplain at Adams County Detention Facility, certified American Correctional Chaplain, spiritual director and on-call hospital chaplain. She founded the Transformation

Project Prison Ministry (TPPM) in 2005 and founded GriefPathway Ventures, LLC in 2010 to help others learn how to process grief and healing. She also is the founder of Veterans Twofish Foundation, a 501(c)(3) non-profit, in 2011.

Education:
- Multnomah Bible College, B.A.B.E. (1984)
- Iliff School of Theology, Master of Divinity (2002)

Books and Audio Books by Yong Hui V. McDonald:
- *Moment by Moment*
- *Journey With Jesus, Visions, Dreams, Meditations & Reflections*
- *Dancing in the Sky, A Story of Hope for Grieving Hearts*
- *Twisted Logic, The Shadow of Suicide*
- *Twisted Logic, The Window of Depression*
- *Dreams & Interpretations, Healing from Nightmares*
- *I Was The Mountain, In Search of Faith & Revival*
- *The Ultimate Parenting Guide, How to Enjoy Peaceful Parenting and Joyful Children*
- *Prisoners Victory Parade, Extraordinary Stories of Maximum Saints & Former Prisoners*
- *Four Voices, How They Affect Our Minds*
- *Tornadoes, Grief, Loss, Trauma, PTSD & TLT Model for Healing*
- Compiled and published five *Maximum Saints* books under the Transformation Project Prison Ministry.

DVDs produced by Yong Hui:
- *Dancing in The Sky, Mismatched Shoes*
- *Tears of The Dragonfly, Suicide and Suicide Prevention* (Audio CD is also available)

Spanish books produced by Yong Hui:
- *Twisted Logic, The Shadow of Suicide*
- *Journey With Jesus, Visions, Dreams, Meditations & Reflections*
GriefPathway Ventures, LLC., P.O. Box 220, Brighton, CO 80601
Website: www.griefpathway.com, Email: griefpwv@gmail.com

www.ingramcontent.com/pod-product-compliance
Lightning Source LLC
Chambersburg PA
CBHW060805050426
42449CB00008B/1544

9780982555149